Carving Santas from Around the World

by Cyndi Joslyn-Carhart

Fox Chapel Publishing
1970 Broad Street • East Petersburg, PA 17520
www.FoxChapelPublishing.com

Publisher	Alan Giagnocavo
Book Editor	Ayleen Stellhorn
Cover Design	Tim Mize
Desktop Specialist	Leah Smirlis

ISBN 1–56523–187-2
Library of Congress Preassigned Card Number: 2003107181

To order your copy of this book,
please send check or money order
for the cover price plus $3.50 shipping to:
Fox Chapel Publishing Company, Inc.
Book Orders
1970 Broad St.
East Petersburg, PA 17520

Or visit us on the web at **www.FoxChapelPublishing.com**

Manufactured in China
10 9 8 7 6 5 4 3 2

DEDICATION

To Jenna
May you too find and live your heart's desire

To Jeff
For providing safe harbor for my heart

ACKNOWLEDGMENTS

Thanks to Jenna, my much loved-daughter, my friend and my most honest and valued critic. She inspires me to do my best work. I can always count on her love and support. She is always there with an honest appraisal and the encouragement to persevere until I get it just right.

Thanks to my husband, Jeff, for his love, support and encouragement. He has graciously accepted my working late into the night and through entire weekends. He was good-natured about uninspired meals and overlooked an abundance of woodchips throughout the house to afford me the opportunity to fulfill my desire to create this book.

Thanks to my friends Gayle and John Salisbury, who for years encouraged me through the idea stage of the book and helped me find the confidence and courage to actually manifest the idea.

Thanks to Jim Joslyn for showing me how to make my written words mean what they say.

Thanks to Ayleen Stellhorn for giving me a little more time.

Thanks to Vila, XiChel, Archangel Michael and all the others for their divine inspiration and guidance.

And, finally, thank you to my wonderful Missoula Carvers: Nora Bradley, Deb Beaudette, Dorothy Dorville, Lynn Dukelow, Karen Gologoski, Joyce Jacobsen, Barb Johnson, Elaine Kohler, Don Murray, Pam Okland, Jim Reid, Dian Schmidt, Betty Toczek, Rita Tucker and the many others who moved in and out of our carving circle. Thank you for carving with me for nearly a decade, teaching me how to teach, while becoming my dear friends in the process.

About the Author

Cyndi Joslyn-Carhart is a professional woodcarver who lives in Arvada, Colorado. During the past several years she has specialized in creating a variety of original Santas, many of which now happily reside in homes throughout the United States. She has also developed a workshop for aspiring Santa carvers of all skill levels. She conducts several of these workshops every year. This book is the outgrowth of, and complement to, those workshops. Additional information about Cyndi, her workshops and places to get specialty items for Santa carving can be found at her website: *www.cyndijoslyn-carhart.com.*

Table of Contents

Introduction

Have you ever been stumped after buying a how-to book or pattern? Were you unable to satisfactorily complete a project because the instructions were vague? Was the project too complicated?

Well, here are some projects that you can easily undertake and complete!

The instructions in *Carving Santas From Around the World* are clear and concise, and they're photographically illustrated from the carver's perspective to help make them readily understood.

So, whether you have no carving experience or are a skilled professional, gather your tools around you and enjoy the charm and appeal of the carving process, as well as the Santas you are about to create. You will need to focus a little bit (a great stress reliever), you will be entertained, and you can bring forth your sense of whimsical creativity.

Enjoy,

Cyndi Joslyn-Carhart

Getting Started

part one

Carving requires quality materials and tools to achieve a satisfactory product. Acquiring these items is the first step in the actual carving process. So let's start with what you need and where to get it.

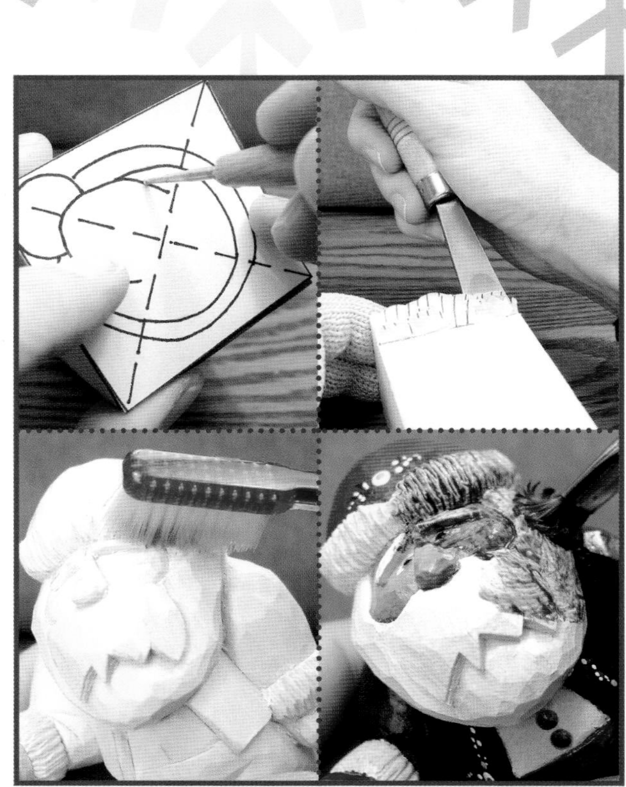

•part one•

Carving Basics

A few well-selected, quality tools will serve you far better and longer than a budget-priced starter set. Quality tools stay sharp longer, and sharp tools are the hallmark of comfortable, quality carving. The basic tools you'll need for carving the Santas in this book are pictured from top to bottom in Figure 1.

- ★ Cutting knife (such as the Flexcut KN-12)
- ★ Detail knife (such as the Flexcut KN-13)
- ★ #3 x ⅞" palm gouge (such as Flexcut FR-700 or Woodcraft #08W31)

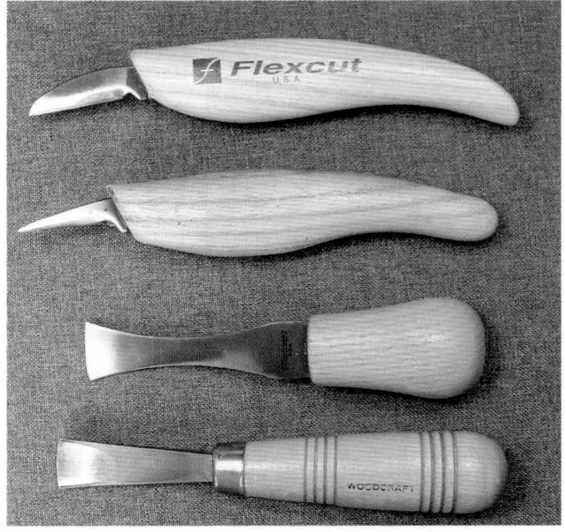
Flexcut

Figure 1: All the Santas in this book can be carved with three tools (from top to bottom): a carving knife (such as the Flexcut™ KN-12), a detail knife (such as the Flexcut™ KN-13), and a #3 x ⅞in. palm gouge (such as the Flexcut™ FR-700 or the Woodcraft™ #08W31).

Note that the cutting edge of a gouge is curved to assist in scooping out sections of wood. The degree of curve is denoted by a number: The lower the number, the less the curve; the higher the number the greater the curve. So, for example, a #9 gouge has more of a curve than a #5 gouge. (See Figure 2.)

Figure 2: Gouges come in a variety of sizes and shapes. A smaller number in the gouge's description denotes less of a curve than a higher number. For example, the gouge on the bottom is a #5; the gouge on the top is a #9.

Some other tools, which will make the carving process more convenient and give you the ability to add specialty touches to your carvings, are pictured top to bottom in Figure 3.

- ★ 3 mm, #5 gouge
- ★ 10 mm, #9 gouge
- ★ 6 mm, #7 gouge
- ★ 8 mm, #12 v-tool

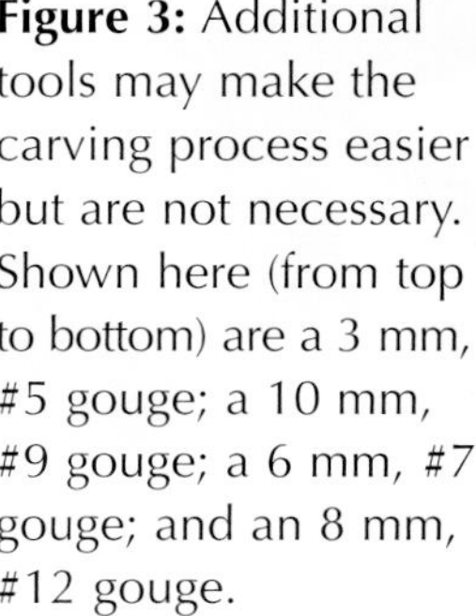

Figure 3: Additional tools may make the carving process easier but are not necessary. Shown here (from top to bottom) are a 3 mm, #5 gouge; a 10 mm, #9 gouge; a 6 mm, #7 gouge; and an 8 mm, #12 gouge.

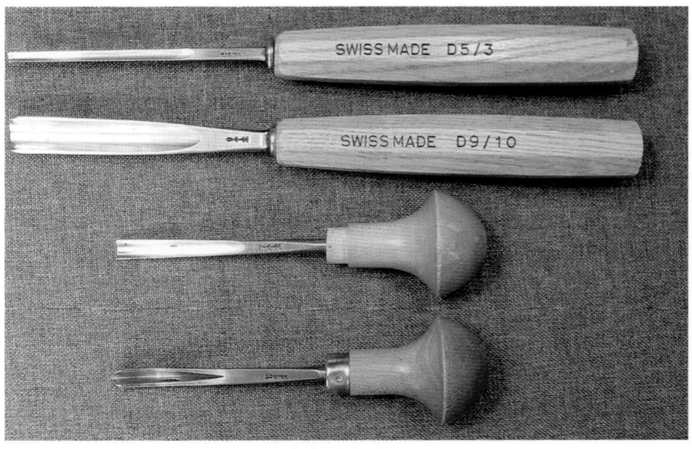
SWISS MADE D5/3
SWISS MADE D9/10

Keeping Tools Sharp

To keep your tools in razor-sharp condition, you'll need to strop them regularly with a strop or a slipstrop. The rule of thumb is five minutes of stropping for every 30 minutes of carving.

For knives, use a paddle-shaped strop made of a piece of wood covered with leather. Holding the blade almost flat against the leather, slowly stroke the blade up the length of the strop 50 times, then down the length of the strop 50 times. Remember, always strop away from the cutting edge of the knife. If you strop in the direction of the cutting edge, the blade will cut into the leather. (See the sidebar.)

For gouges, use a specialty strop (such as a slipstrop from Flexcut™), which has a variety of rounded surfaces to conform and hone the different inside curves of gouges. Strop the outside of the tool first. Place a portion of the outside curve of the gouge on the strop, then pull the gouge toward you over the length of the strop. Repeat this action 50 times, rolling the edge of the gouge slightly each time to polish the entire surface of the blade. Then place the inside curve of the gouge over the curved part of the specialty strop. Pull the gouge toward you 50 times, making sure that all areas of the blade come into contact with the leather as you strop. (See the sidebar on page 4.)

Stropping a Knife

Strop your knife for five minutes after every 30 minutes of carving to keep the edge honed and sharp.

With the cutting edge facing you, lay the blade flat on the strop.

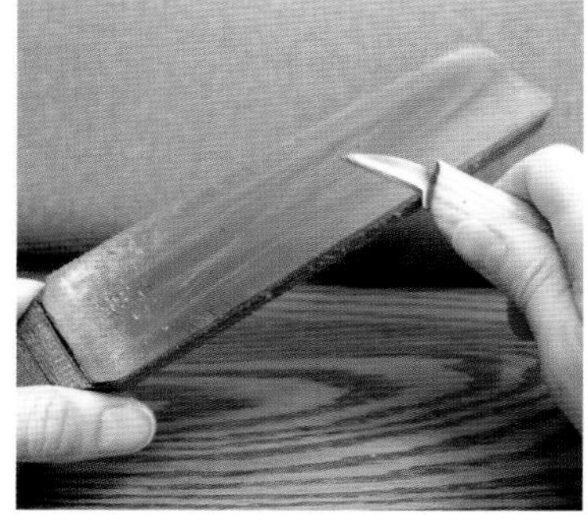

Push the blade away from you. Repeat 50 times.

Turn the cutting edge away from you.

Pull the knife toward you. Repeat 50 times.

STROPPING A GOUGE

Frequent stropping of gouges will keep the cutting edges in top carving condition.

Place the outside edge of the gouge on the strop at an angle. Face the cutting edge away from you.

Pull the gouge toward you.

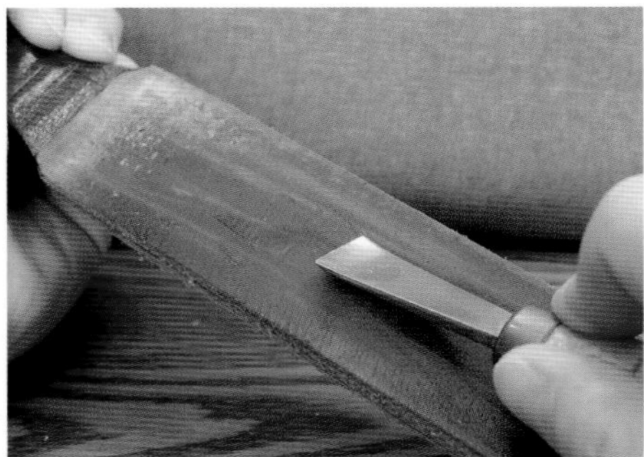

Roll the cutting edge slightly as you reach the end of the strop.

Switch to a curved specialty strop.

Pull the gouge toward you. Repeat 50 times.

Other Supplies

With the sharp tools used to carve, it's sometimes easy to nick fingers or clothes. I recommend wearing either a leather apron or a canvas apron with a leather patch and a slash-proof carving glove. In addition to these safety supplies, there are other supplies that you should have before you begin carving. You may already have most of these items around your house.

- ★ Flexible,12" ruler (my favorite is a 2"-wide clear quilting ruler)
- ★ Pencil
- ★ Carbon or graphite paper
- ★ Painting supplies (discussed in further detail in the painting section)
- ★ Tissue paper for tracing patterns
- ★ Wood repair epoxy putty (such as Quikwood™) and/or Carpenter's™ wood filler
- ★ Fine grain (#100 grit) sandpaper or sandpaper stick
- ★ Stylus
- ★ Instant glue (such as Superglue™)

Some Santas require the following:

- ★ 2 bar clamps or spring clamps with at least a 3" capacity
- ★ 24-gauge brass wire
- ★ Carpenter's wood glue
- ★ Brass eye pins (found in the jewelry findings section of a craft store)
- ★ 1⁄16" drill bit
- ★ Sandwich picks

Wood

Basswood is my carving wood of choice. It's classified as a hardwood, but it's one of the softer hardwoods. It has very even grain and holds detail well. Some carvers prefer sugar pine, and that is acceptable. However, some sugar pine is so soft that, unless your tools are razor sharp, the wood can get mushy and you can easily lose details. Basswood is more forgiving of tools that are not razor sharp.

A wood list, included in the pattern section, shows you what sizes of wood you need for each Santa. All of the wood pieces can be easily cut with a handsaw or a coping saw from 2 in. or 3 in. wood stock.

Understanding wood grain is an important part of carving, and the best way to learn about wood grain is to actually begin carving. When you carve with the grain of the wood, the tool moves through the wood smoothly, creating little wood curls. The tool will naturally rise to the surface of the wood. Try carving in the opposite direction or against the grain. The tool seems to dig deeper into the wood, and the action feels rough. The surface you carve may also be jagged, and you will produce wood "hairies" instead of wood curls.

If you are carving with the grain, the knife will cut easily through the wood, creating wood curls.

If you are carving against the grain, the knife will resist cutting, creating "hairies."

Pattern Use

The patterns in this book may look a bit unusual, but they have proven to be quite easy to use by the students in my Santa carving classes. Instead of providing my students with finished front, side and top views, I provide them with wrap-around patterns showing the basic cuts. These patterns are perfect for beginners, because they show exactly how much wood needs to be removed.

To use the wrap-around patterns, simply follow the directions below. Keep in mind that proper alignment of the patterns on the block is very important.

To Transfer a Pattern

1. Cut out a 2" by 2" square of carbon or graphite paper.
2. Cut out an 8" x 3¼" rectangle of carbon or graphite paper.
3. Trace a pattern from the book onto tissue paper.
4. Cut out the top and bottom pattern sections.
5. Cut out the body pattern section.
6. Mark "front" and "back" on the wood. Wrap the carbon or graphite paper around the block with the carbon side toward the block.
7. Lay the pattern over the carbon paper, matching up the front, back and corner edges of the wood.
8. With a pencil or stylus trace the pattern lines onto the wood.
9. Place a 2" by 2" square of carbon paper on top of the block with the carbon toward the block. Lay the "top" pattern piece over the carbon paper, matching the front of the pattern to the front of the block of wood.
10. With a pencil or stylus trace the pattern lines onto the wood.
11. Repeat the procedure for the bottom of the wood, remembering to align the pattern front to the wood front.

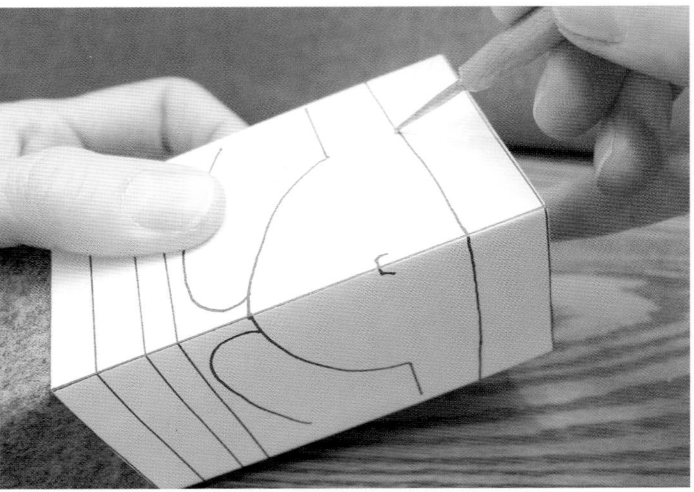

Trace the front, back and side view patterns onto the wood.

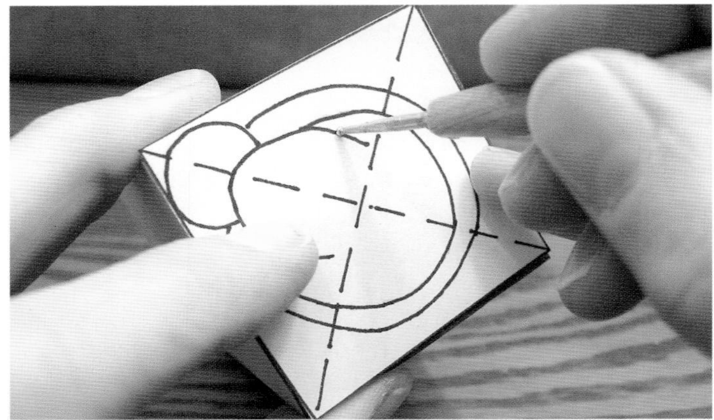

Trace the top view pattern (shown here) and the bottom view pattern onto the wood.

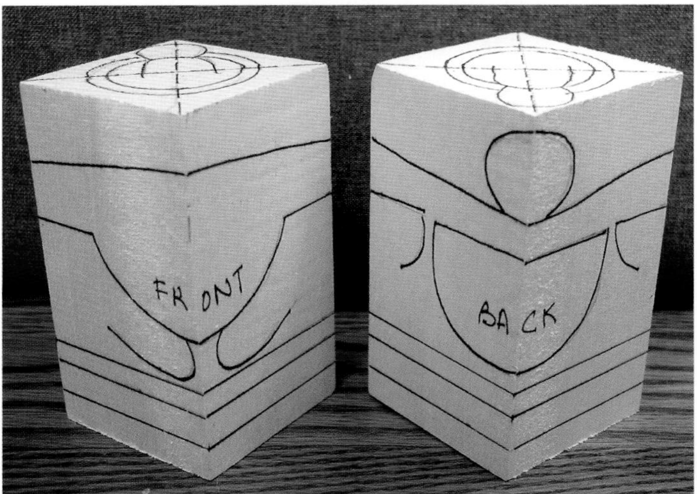
FR ONT
BA CK

The block is ready to be carved.

•part one•

Basic Cuts

All of the Santas in this book are carved with two basic cuts: the stop cut and a slicing cut to the stop cut.

The stop cut is made by pulling the sharp edge of the cutting knife along the solid lines that you have traced on the wood. This is called "scoring" the wood. Start at one edge and continue across the line until you are about ¼ in. from the opposite edge of the wood. Then, from the opposite edge, score back to meet the score line you just created. Your score line should be about 1⁄16 in. deep. You may want to score the line a couple of times to reach a depth of ⅛ in.

Now, with a gouge, or a knife, shave away a thin layer of wood up to the score line. This is called "carving back to the stop cut." The score line naturally interrupts the forward motion of the gouge—hence the term "stop cut." This thin layer of wood may fall right off your block. If it doesn't, turn the block of wood around and push the gouge or knife into the wood retracing the score line. This will remove the thin layer of wood and begins to create a ledge. Continue to carve off thin layers of wood until you have removed all the wood in the shaded area and created a flat and level ledge.

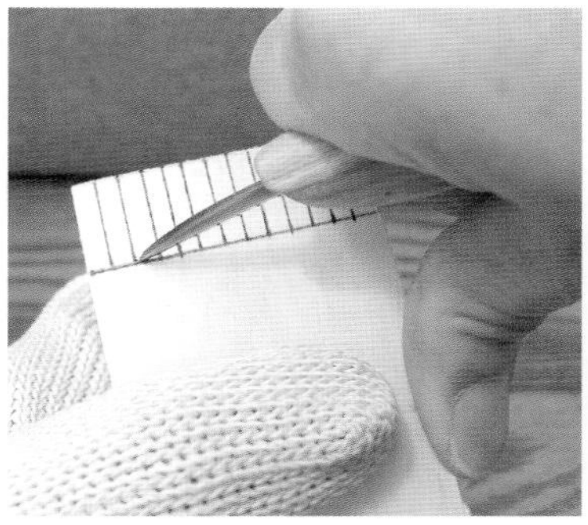

Pull the sharp edge of the cutting knife along the pattern lines to create a stop cut.

Shave away a thin layer of wood up to the stop cut.

Continue removing thin layers of wood until a shelf is created.

Painting Basics

First, let's review the painting supplies you will need. Specific paint colors are marked on the color charts for each individual Santa and are simply a suggestion. I encourage you to personalize the Santas in any way you wish, and paint is the perfect way to do just that. Many of the Santas have little floral doodad borders around the bottoms of their coats or floral doodad motifs on their hats. Doodads are really very easy to paint and offer you another option for personalizing your Santa.

Paint

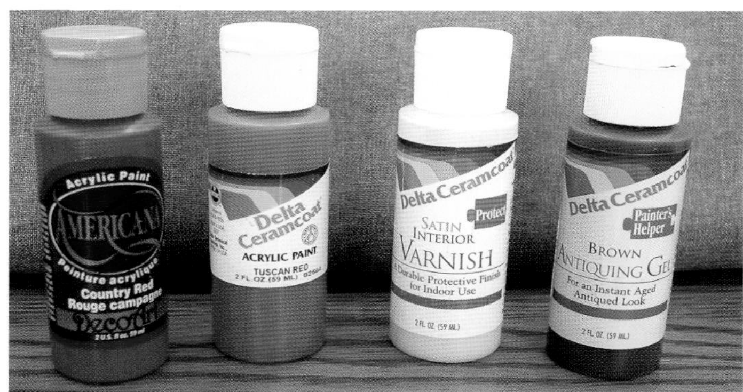
Acrylic Paint
Americana
Peinture acrylique
Country Red
Rouge campagne
DecoArt
Delta Ceramcoat
ACRYLIC PAINT
TUSCAN RED
Delta Ceramcoat
Protect
Satin Interior Varnish
Durable Protective Finish for Indoor Use
Delta Ceramcoat
Painter's Helper
Brown Antiquing Gel
For an Instant Aged Antiqued Look

To paint the Santas in this book, you'll need the following:

- 2 oz. bottles of acrylic paint (specific colors are noted in the directions)
- 2 oz. bottle of water-based varnish (such as Delta Ceramcoat Satin Interior Varnish)
- 2 oz. bottle of brown antiquing gel (such as Delta Ceramcoat Antiquing Gel)

Brushes

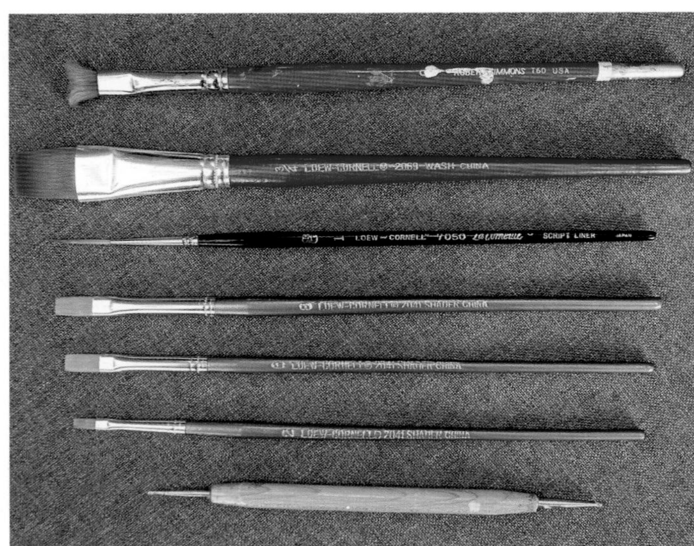

Brushes are an important part of painting. Buy the best brushes you can afford. Pictured from top to bottom:

For antiquing—a worn out flat brush size 8 or 10
For varnishing—a ¾in. flat wash brush
For painting eyes— a #0 or #1 liner brush
For base coating—flat (shader) brushes, synthetic and suitable for use with acrylic paint, in sizes #8, #6, #2
For tiny doodad dots—a stylus or toothpick

Miscellaneous Items

In addition to the paints and brushes, you'll also need the items on the following list:

Newspaper
Wax paper
Water jar or water basin with brush holder
Paper towels
#100 grit sand paper or sandpaper stick
old toothbrush
Antiquing rags such as old white t-shirts
Cotton swabs
Toothpicks

Prepare Your Painting Area

Cover your painting area with newspaper. Put a sheet of wax paper off to the side. Any Santas waiting to dry will be placed here. Fold another piece of wax paper in half for puddles of paint. A paper towel close by is very convenient for drying brushes as you remove them from the water jar.

Wax paper and newspaper help to keep your painting area neat and clean.

An old toothbrush can be used to remove wood fibers from the project's surface.

The more you sand, the less the carved facets of the piece will show. I do very little sanding, because I like the look the knife cuts give the finished piece.

After you finish carving, scrub the Santa with an old, dry toothbrush to remove any tiny wood fibers that may be stuck in cracks or crevices. I do very little sanding before I start painting. This allows the carving facets to show.

Now you're ready to paint. Follow the painting demonstration on the following pages to see my suggestions for painting the Santas in this book. Of course, these are just suggestions. You may already have a favorite way to paint your projects.

Painting Santa

I've often heard it said that painting can make or break a carving, but there's really no need to be wary of painting your Santa. The painting techniques are really very simple.

Start the painting process with Santa's face. Paint two coats of medium flesh color over the entire face, including the eyebrows. Make sure you get paint into all the little cracks and creases. After the first coat of paint dries, sand any raised grain with #100 grit

Figure 1. A blush color is blended into the flesh tones of the face with a dry brush.

Figure 2. I believe the eyes create Santa's personality. Take your time and get the eyes just right—and don't forget the highlights. Lifelike eyes will overshadow many other little flaws.

Figure 3. Doodads, painted with a detail brush or stylus, help to personalize your Santa.

Figure 4. Several thin coats of watered-down varnish will help to protect the painted surface.

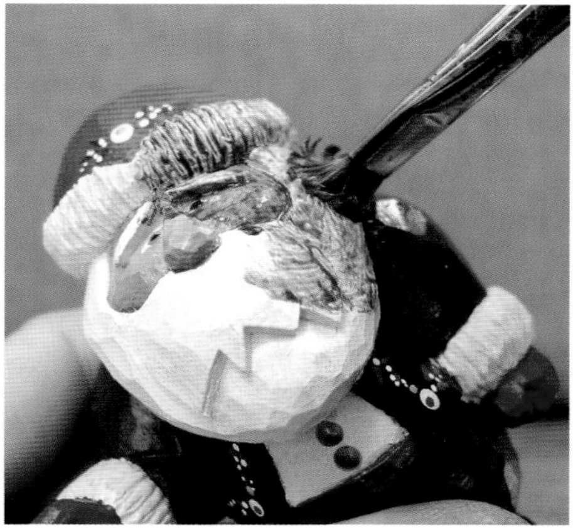

Figure 5. Holding the Santa with a soft cloth will keep your fingers—and fingerprints—out of the gel while you are antiquing the piece.

Figure 6. The carved, painted, varnished and antiqued Santa is ready for gift-giving or display upon your holiday mantel.

sandpaper or a sandpaper stick. It's okay to have a little flesh colored paint stray into the beard area. That can be touched up later.

To add the blush to Santa's cheeks, squeeze out a dime-sized pool of adobe-colored paint onto the piece of folded wax paper. Mix in an equal amount of water to thin the paint and make it into a wash. Apply the paint wash to Santa's cheeks and nose with a #6 flat paintbrush. Again, it's okay to get a little stray color on the beard. After you apply the paint wash, quickly rinse the paintbrush in water and dry it on a paper towel. Then, start next to Santa's eyebrows and pull the dry brush down into the cheek area. Repeat this step all across the face. This further blends the blush. (See Figure 1.) You may need to repeat this process a couple of times before you have the desired amount of blush on Santa's cheeks.

Santa's beard and eyebrows are next. With a #8 flat paintbrush, basecoat the beard area with two coats of light ivory, taking special care to cover completely any stray blush or face paint. Use a #2

Carve a Traditional Santa

Wood List

Body 1 ea. 3¾" x 2" x 2"

Paint List

Adobe
Black
Americana® Country red
Empire gold
Golden brown
Ivory
Light ivory
Medium flesh
Woodland night

The Pattern

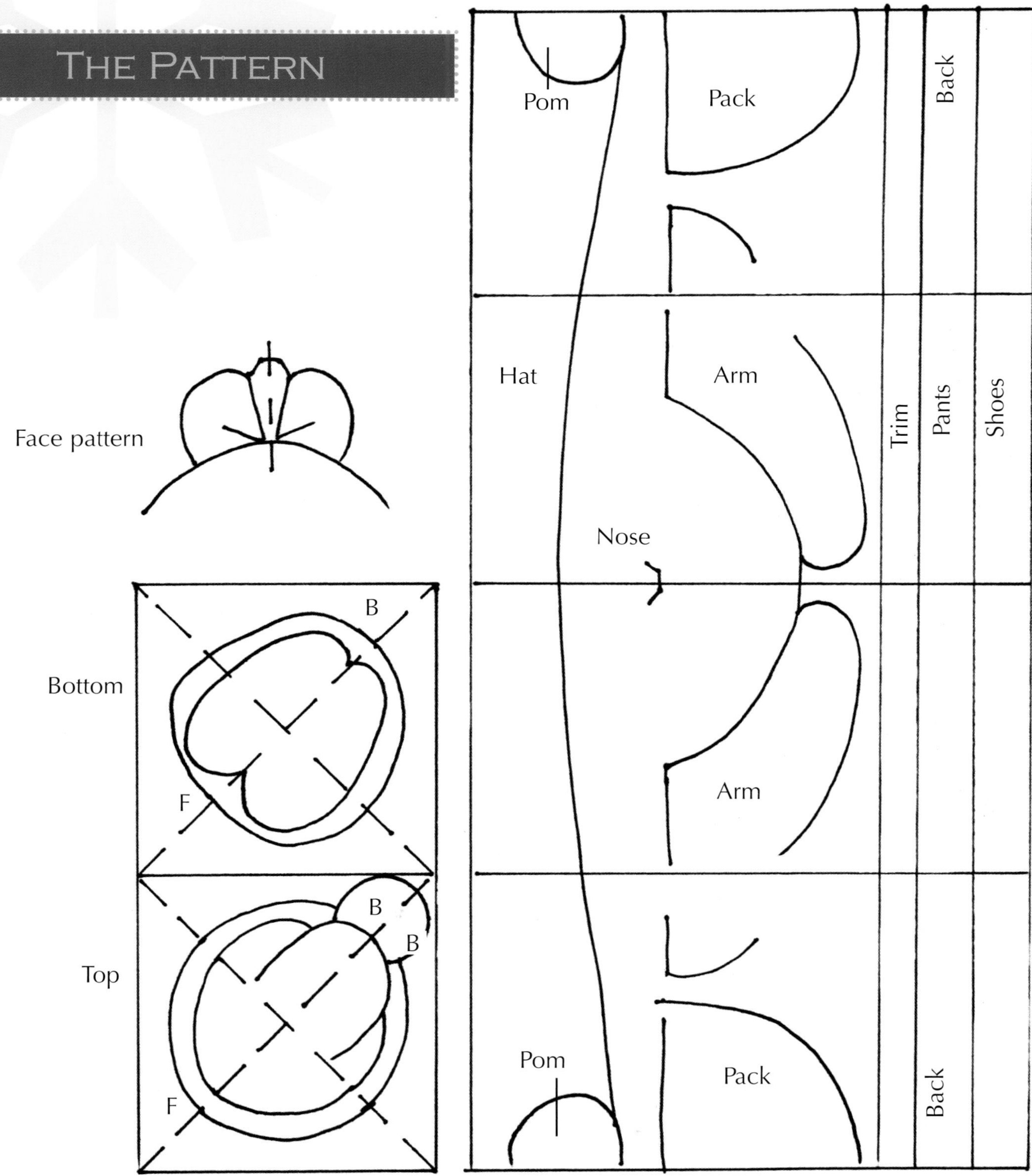

Face pattern
Bottom
B
F
Top
B
B
F
Pom
Pack
Back
Hat
Arm
Trim
Pants
Shoes
Nose
Arm
Pom
Pack
Back

•part two•

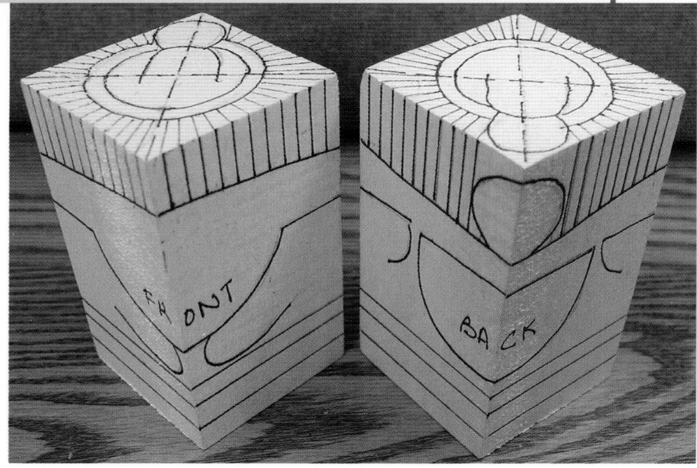
FRONT
BACK

step 1 Your first step is to remove the wood in the shaded hat area.

ONT

step 2 Score the line below the hat.

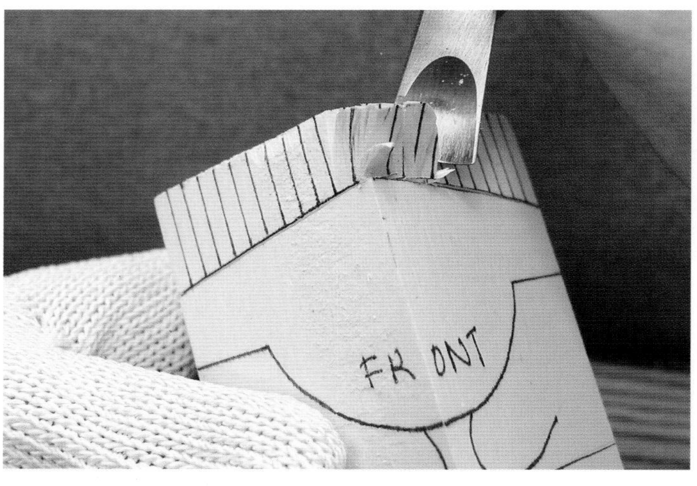
FRONT

step 3 Shave thin layers of wood down to the score line.

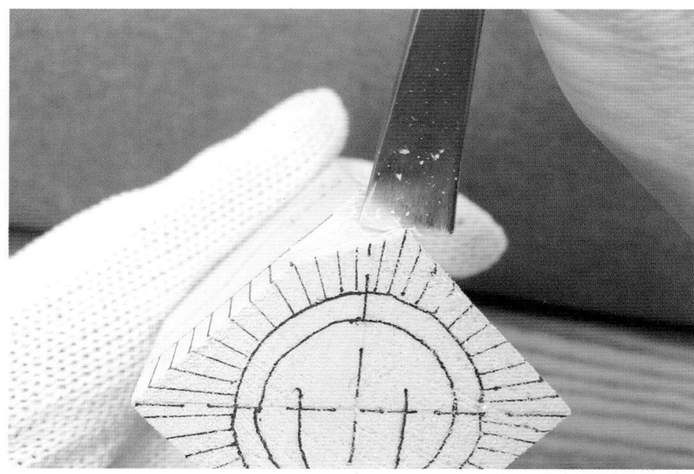

step 4 Recut the score line to remove the slice of wood.

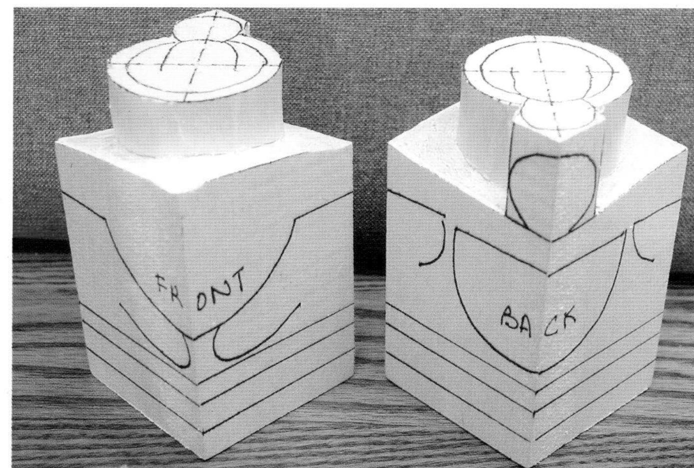
FRONT
BACK

step 5 Continue cutting away thin layers of wood until you have removed all the wood in the shaded area. Be careful not to carve into the pom-pom area on the back of Santa's hat.

ONT

step 6 Next, measure ¼ in. up from the base of the hat in several places around the hat.

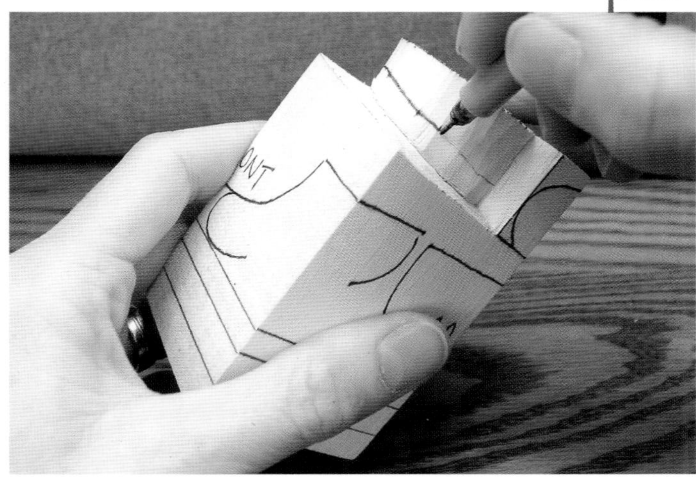

step 7 Connect the marks to form a line ¼ in. above the base of the hat.

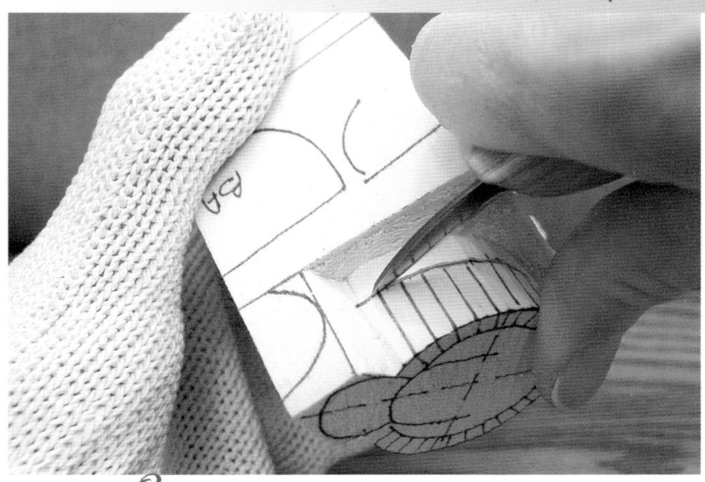

step 8 Score the line you just drew.

step 9 Remove all the wood in the shaded area.

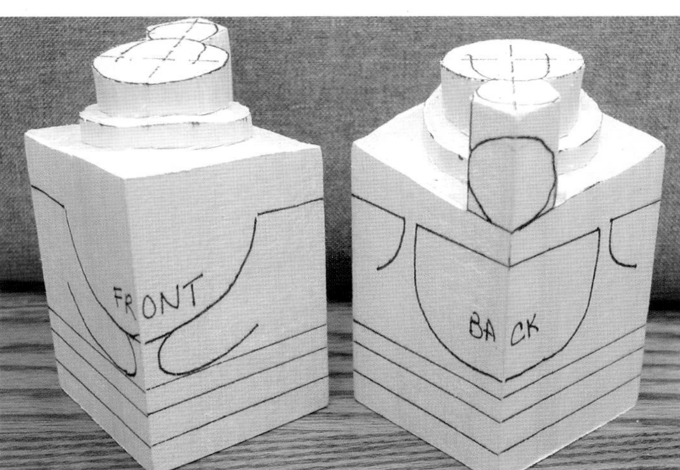
FRONT
BA CK

step 10 The project will look like this.

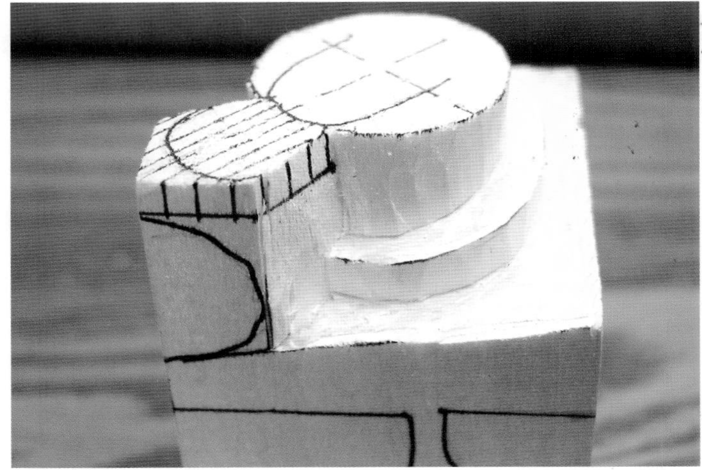

step 11 Turn the project so the back faces you. Draw a parallel line ¼ in. from the top of the wood. This line should rest on the top of the pom-pom circle.

step 12 Score this line and remove the wood in the shaded area by cutting back to the stop cut. Remember to remove only thin layers of wood at a time.

•part two•

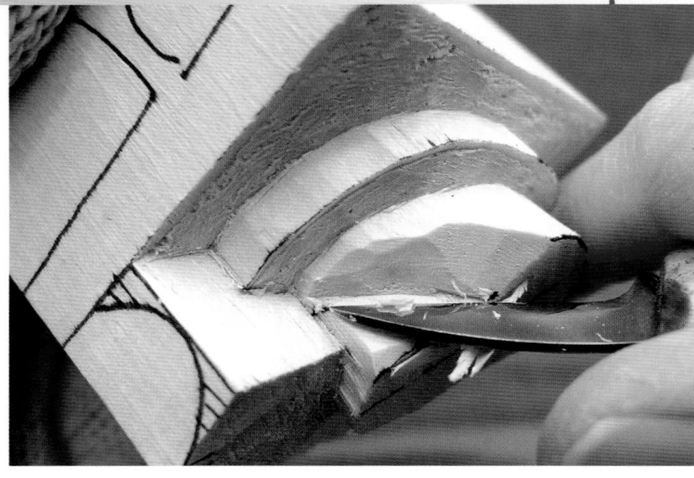

step 13 Score the sides of the hat and carve back up to the score line to create the tail of the hat.

step 14 Score the line directly under the pom-pom.

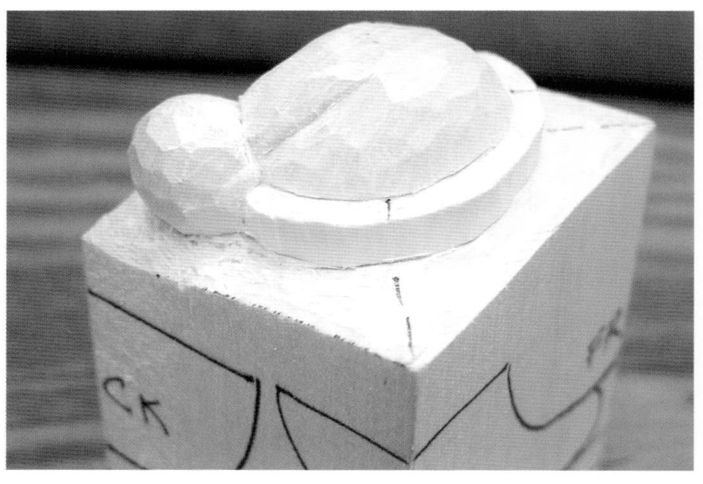
CK

step 15 Begin to round the pom-pom using either the gouge or the cutting knife.

step 16 The wood in the shaded areas above the shoulders will be removed next.

step 17 Push the gouge into the line above the shoulder to create a stop cut on the wood.

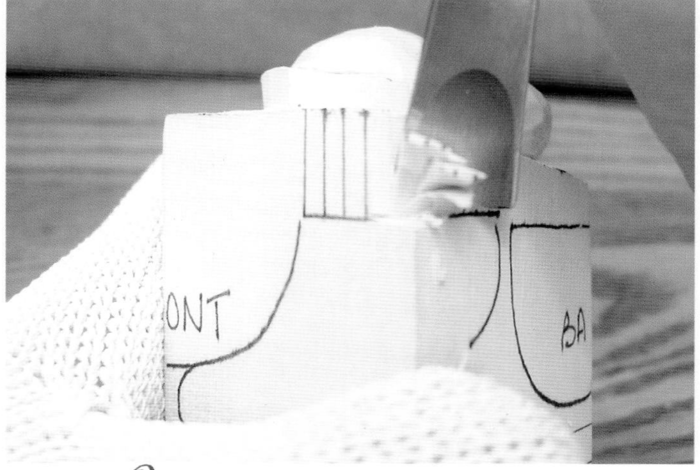
ONT
BA

step 18 Then turn the wood around and carve back down to the stop cut.

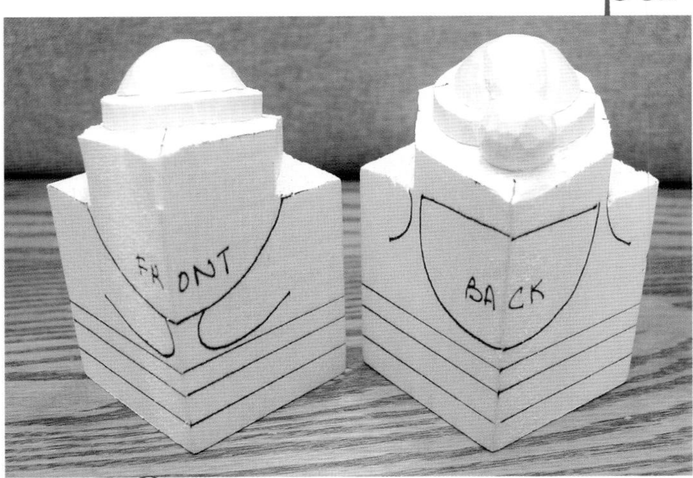
FRONT
BACK

step 19 The progress up to this point.

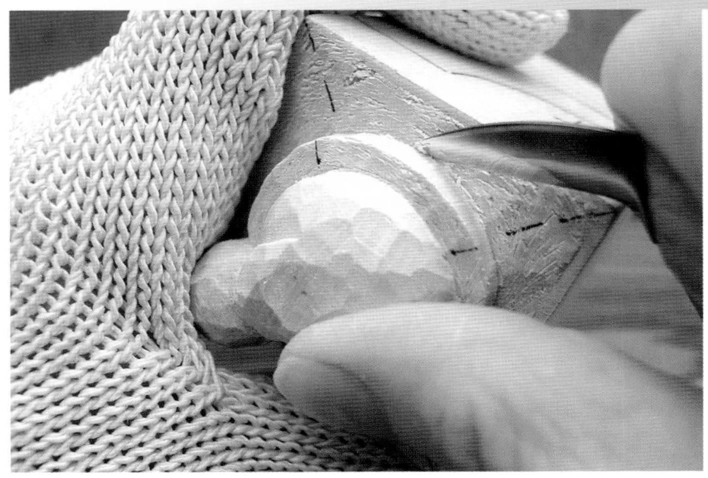

step 20 Score around the bottom of the hat several times.

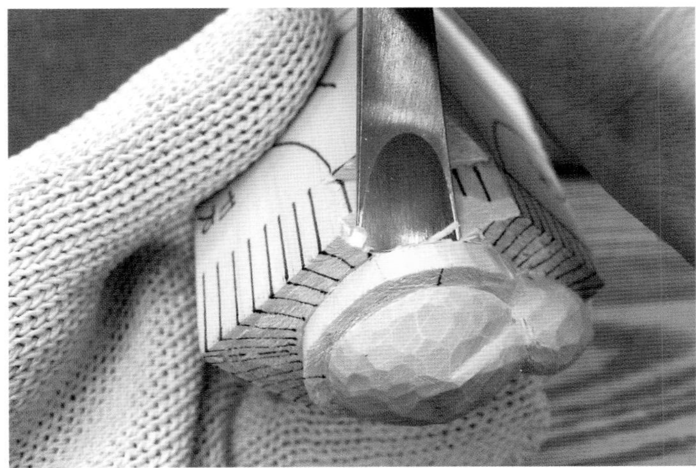

step 21 With a gouge, carve back up to that stop cut in an angled fashion to remove the wood in the shaded area.

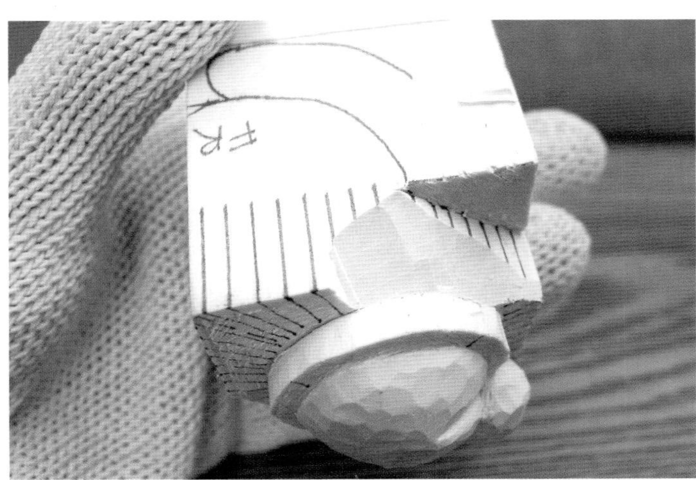

step 22 This cut will pull what will be Santa's head up into his hat.

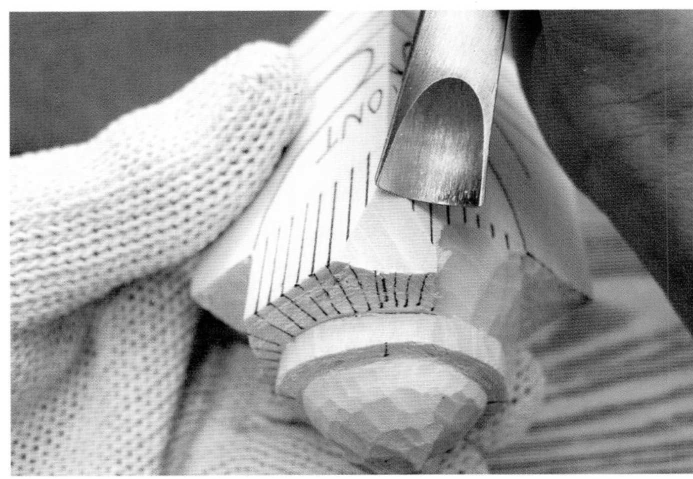

step 23 Carve off the excess wood from the front edge. This will ease the process of pulling the remaining wood up under the hat.

FRONT

step 24 Your goal is to make this area smooth and evenly rounded. Remember, you must take more wood off of the corners to obtain a truly rounded surface.

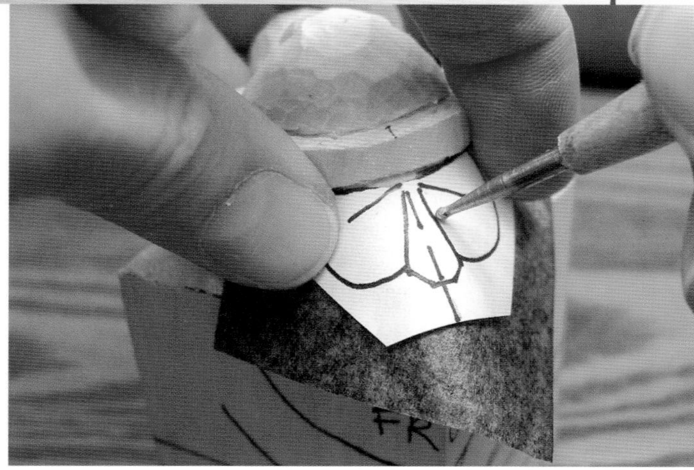
FR

step 25 Trace the face pattern onto the front of Santa below his hat. Align the "center registration line" on Santa to the "face center registration line" of the face pattern.

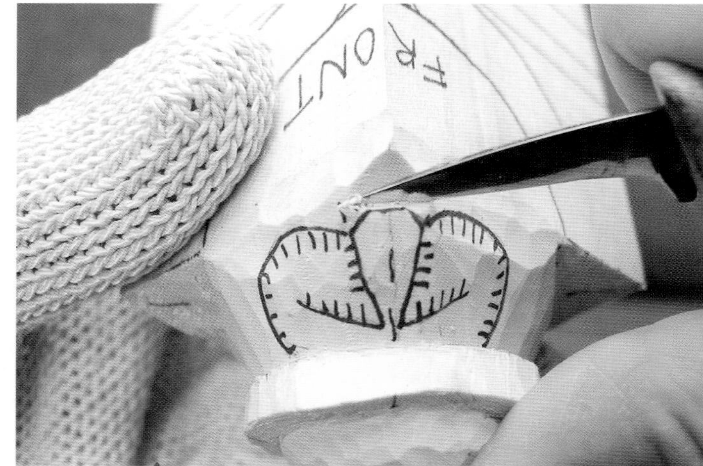
FRONT

step 26 Score the line under Santa's nose and, with the detail knife, carve back to that line, removing a small amount of wood under Santa's nose.

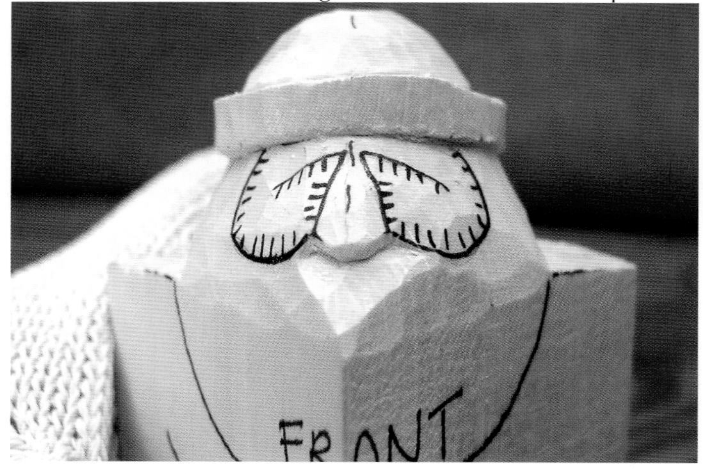
FRONT

step 27 After several cuts to relieve the nose, the face will look like this.

FRONT

step 28 Score all of the solid lines you've traced for Santa's face.

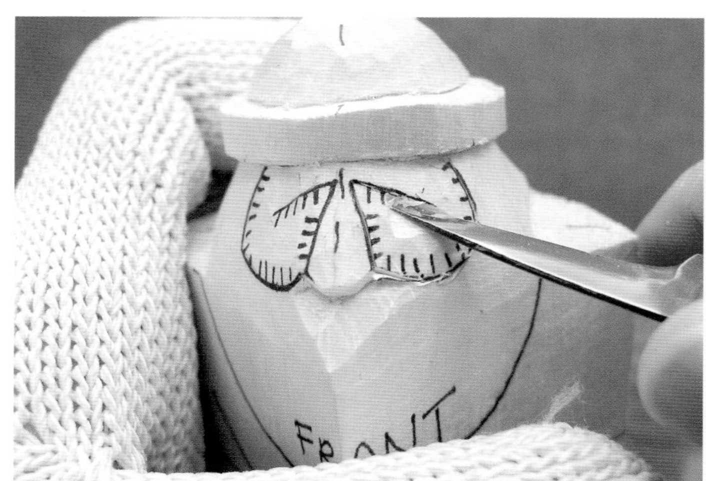
FRONT

step 29 Continuing to use the detail knife, begin removing wood under the eyebrows...

step 30 ...along the sides of the nose and above the beard on the right side of Santa's face.

santa's face

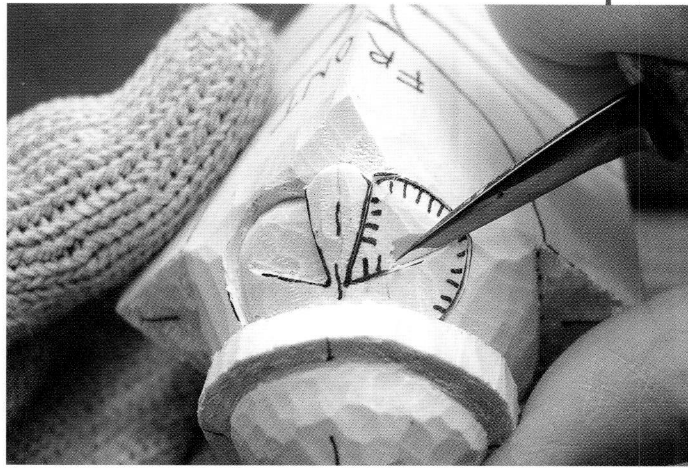
FRONT

step 31 For the left side of the face, turn the piece upside down and carve down to the eyebrow line. Continue to remove wood next to the nose and above the beard line.

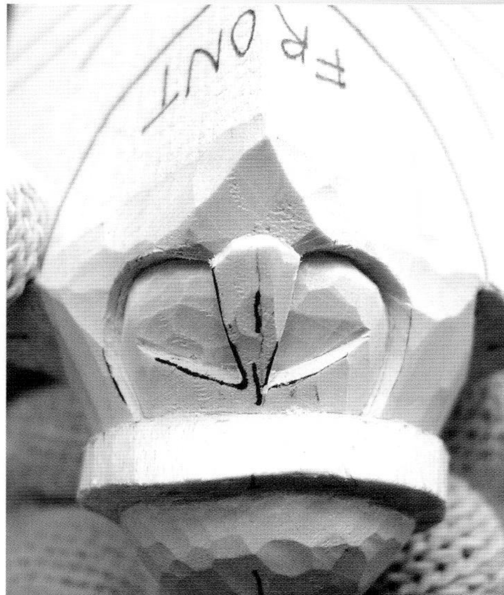
FRONT

step 32 Note the ledge created above the beard as you round the cheeks. From this upside down perspective, make sure the cheeks are equal in depth. Checking this perspective also helps to keep the sides of Santa's face even.

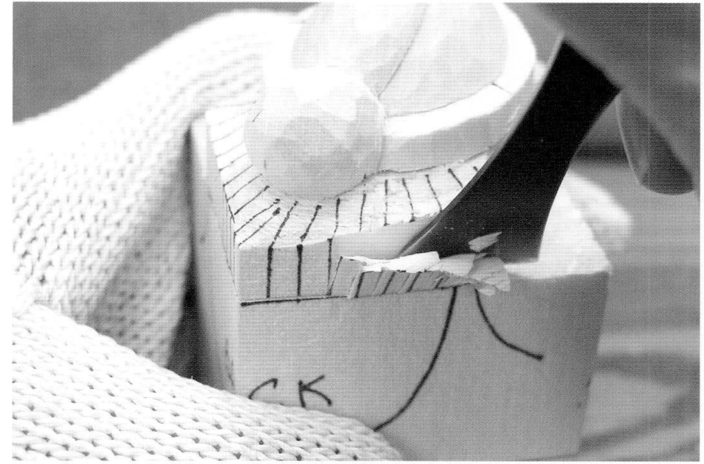

step 33 Remove wood to make a ledge of approximately ¼ in. above the pack on Santa's back.

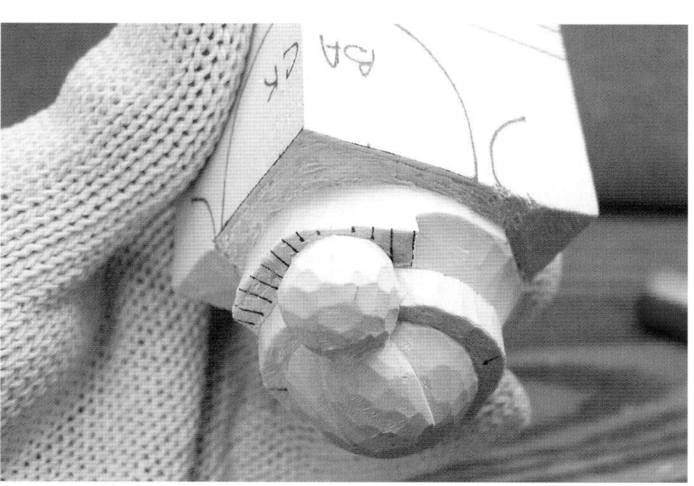

step 34 Continue to remove wood in the same angled fashion as on Santa's face to pull the hair up under his hat.

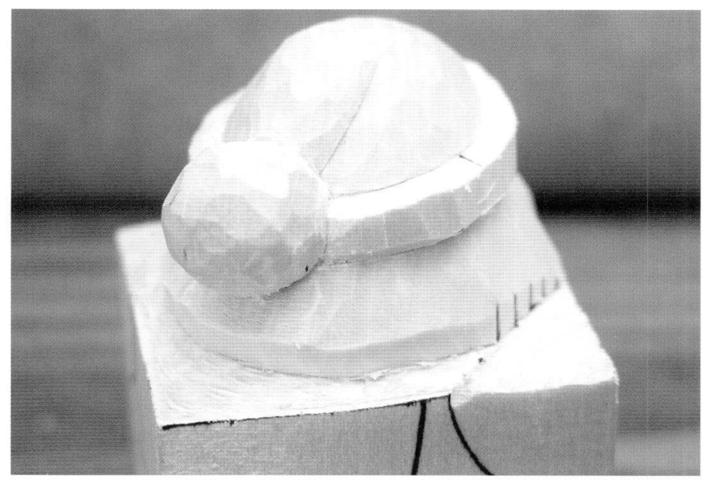

step 35 The progress so far.

santa's boots

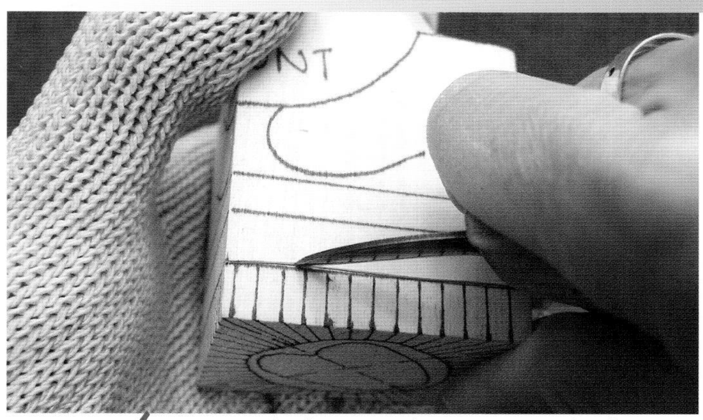

step 36 On the bottom of Santa, score the first line, which is located approximately ⅜ in. above the bottom surface, all the way around Santa. Remove the wood in the shaded area.

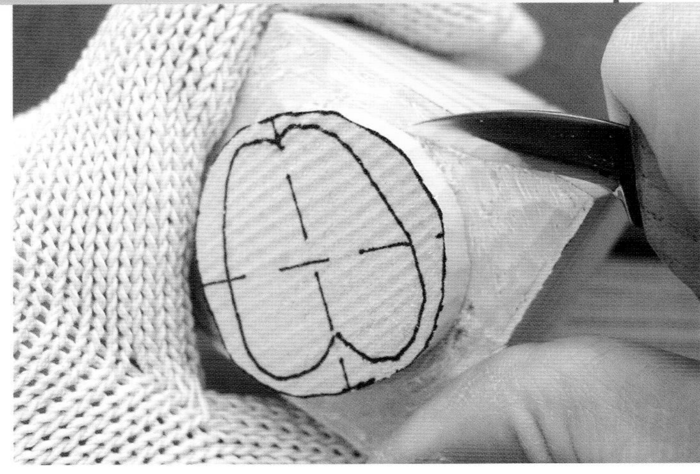

step 37 Progress to this point. Score around the top of the boots next to the body.

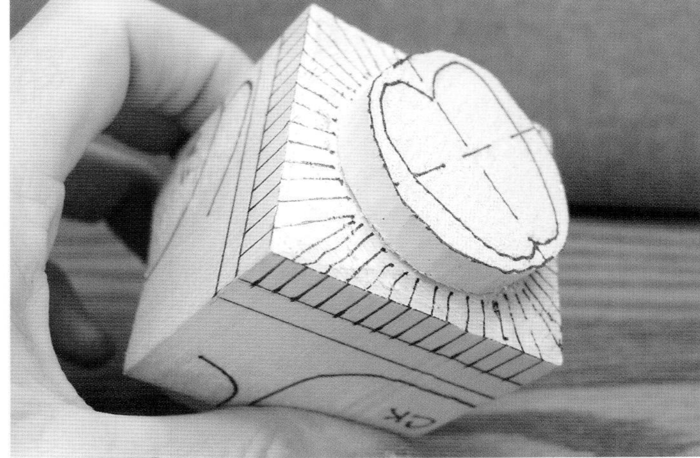

step 38 Score the next line, which is approximately ⅜ in. above the last line.

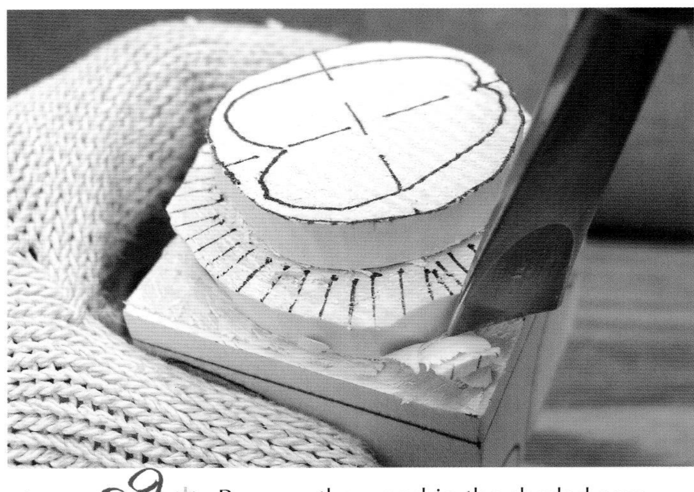

step 39 Remove the wood in the shaded area.

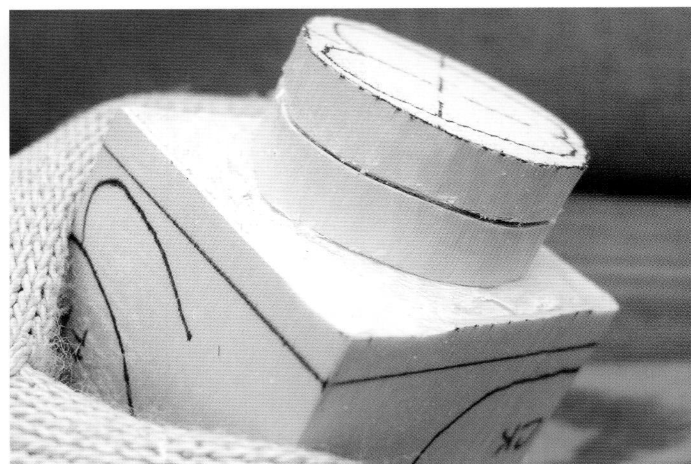

step 40 Your progress should look like this.

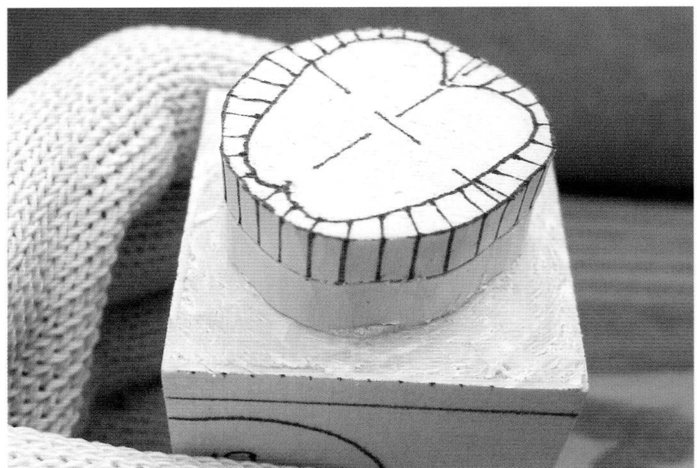

step 41 Remove wood in the shaded area next.

step 42 This further defines the boots.

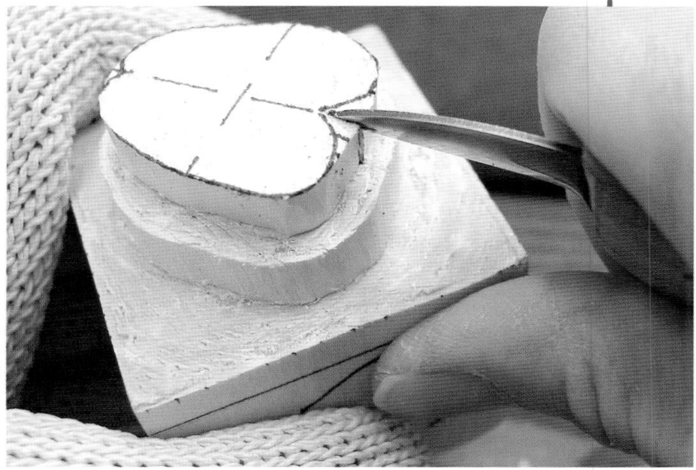

step 43 Score the lines that separate the boots at the front and back. Remove a tiny wedge of wood on both sides of the centerlines. This defines the front and back of each boot.

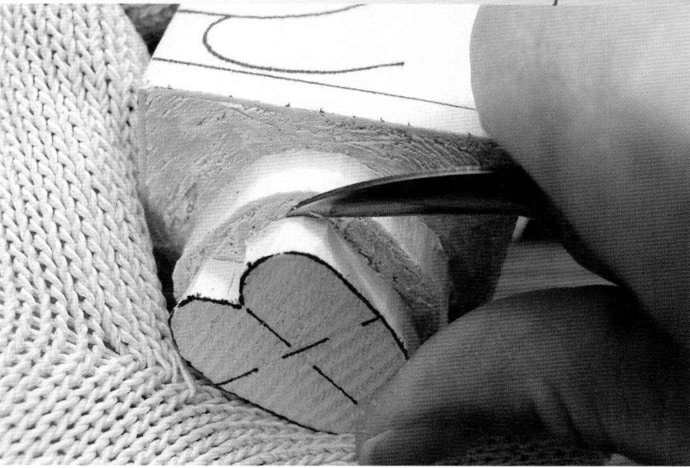

step 44 Score the line above the boots once again.

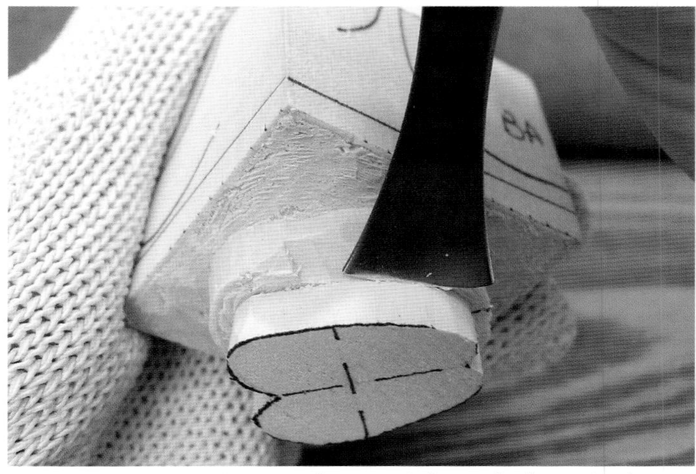
BA

step 45 Remove the wood above the boots in the same angled manner you used to pull Santa's face and the back of his hair up under his hat. This area should be evenly rounded.

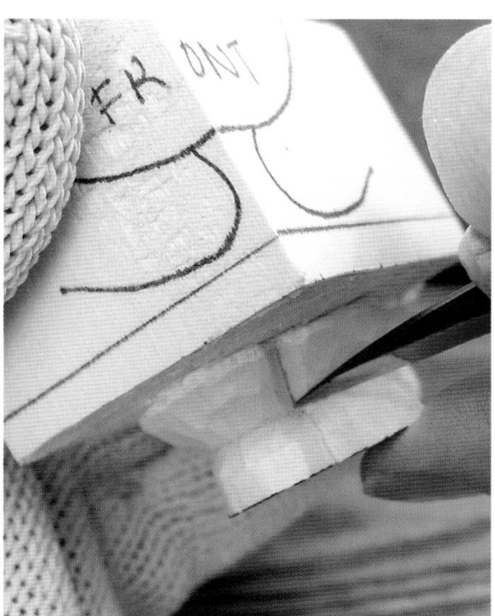
FR ONT

step 46 Redraw the centerline on the pants. Score this line and remove tiny wedges of wood on either side of this centerline to define the pant legs. Use the same technique you used to define the front and back of the boots.

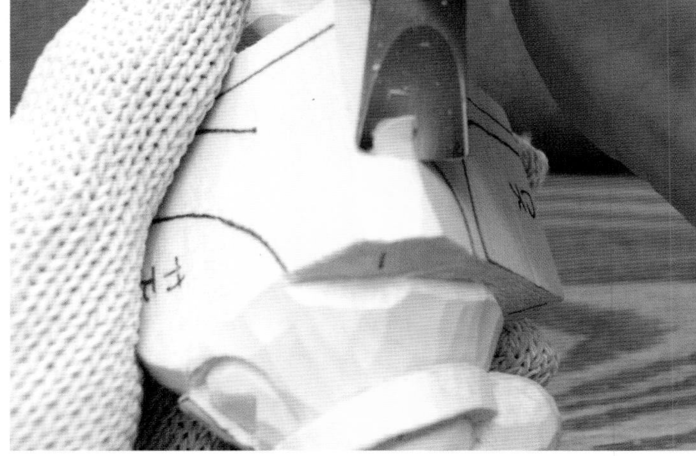

step 47 Round the edges of the wood under each shoulder.

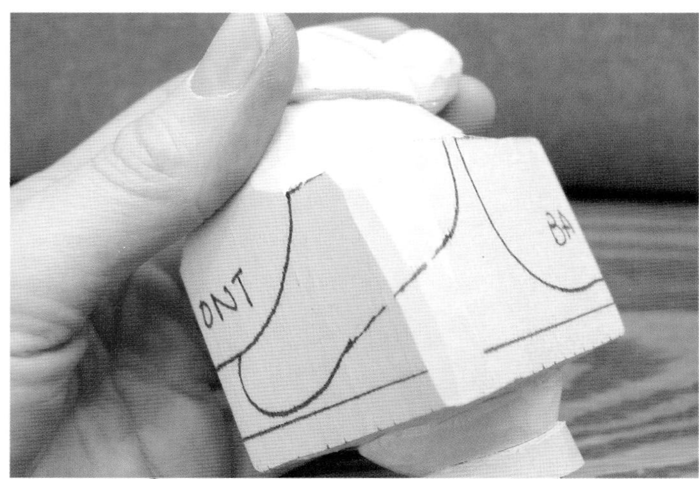
ONT
BA

step 48 Connect the front and back arm lines.

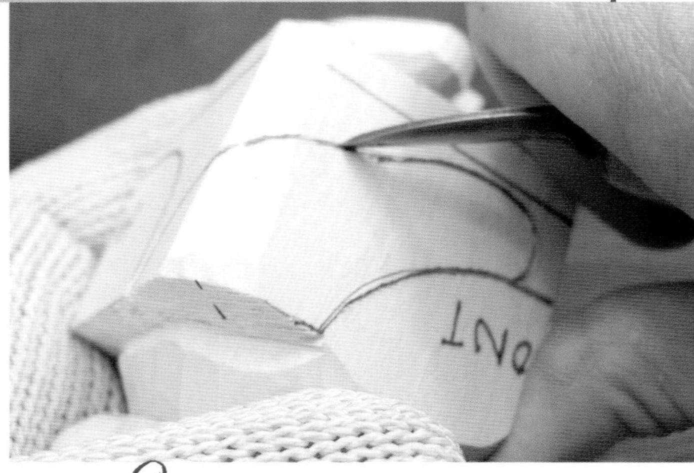

ONT

step 49 Score the lines around Santa's arms and beard.

step 50 Draw a circle on the wood above Santa's boots and pants.

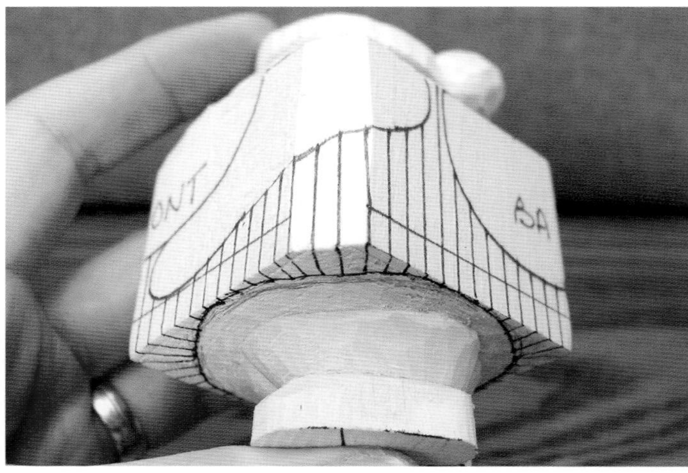

ONT
BA

step 51 Score the line around Santa's pack. The wood in the shaded area will be removed next.

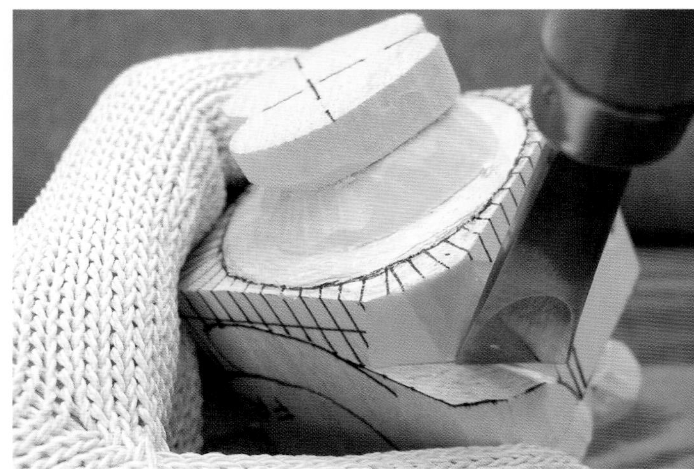

step 52 Using the gouge, remove the wood in the shaded area.

FRONT
BACK

step 53 The progress so far.

santa's arms

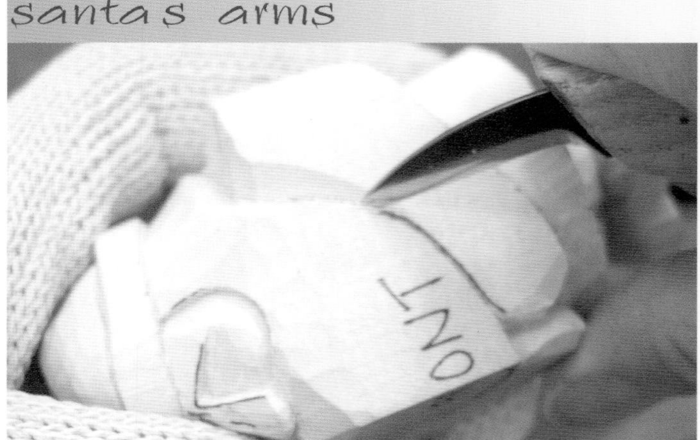

ONT

step 54 With a cutting knife, begin to round the tops of the arms next to Santa's beard.

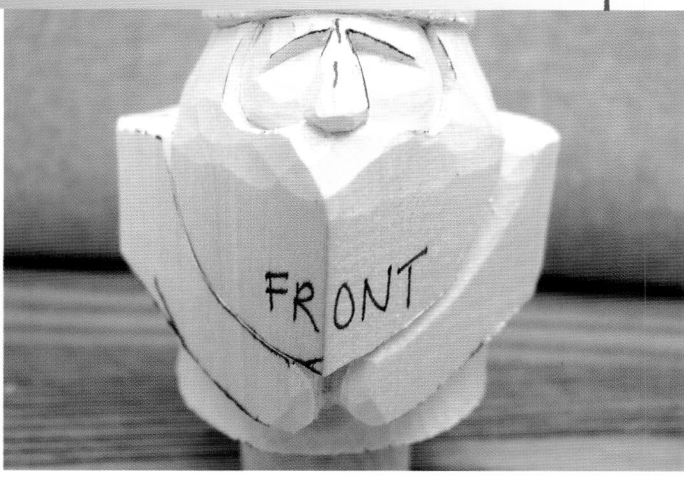
FRONT

step 55 This photo shows the top of one arm completed.

ONT

step 56 The wood in the shaded area will be rounded to shape the shoulders.

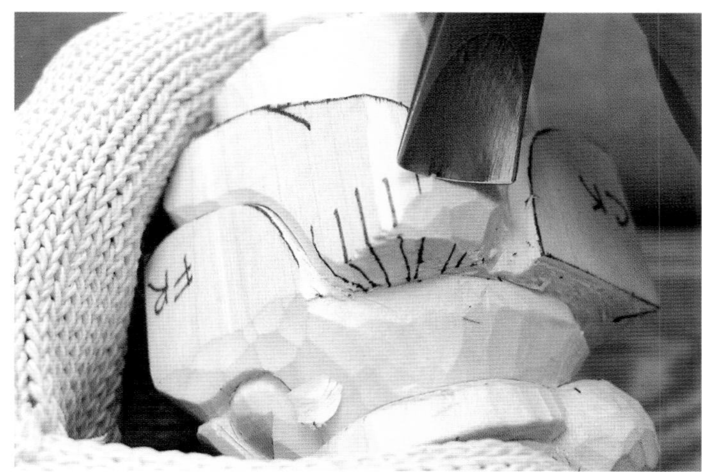

step 57 Use a gouge to round the shoulders.

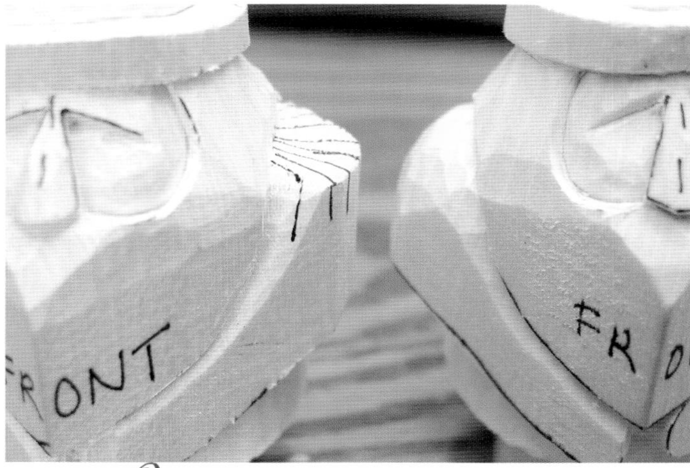
FRONT
FR

step 58 A comparison shows the wood that was removed.

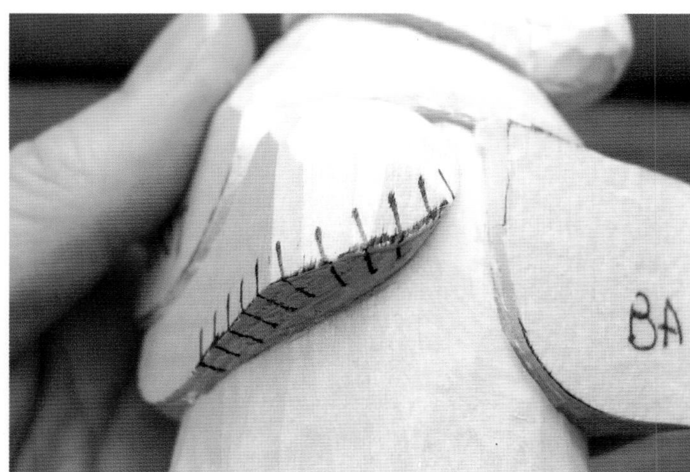
BA

step 59 The wood in the shaded area will be rounded to shape the arms.

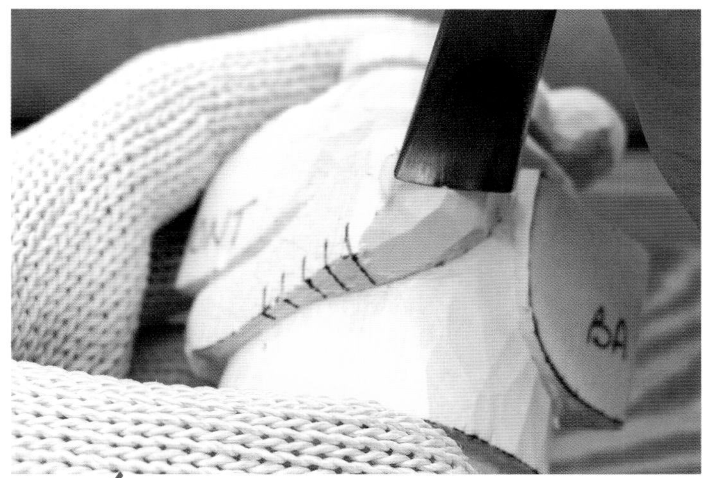
BA

step 60 Continuing with the gouge, round the bottoms of the arms.

santa's arms

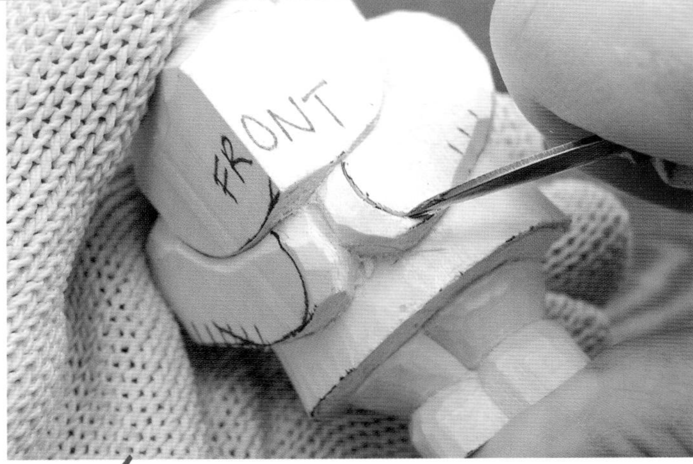
FRONT

step 61 The arms should be approximately 2 in. long. Shorten the length of the arms in the front mitten area if necessary.

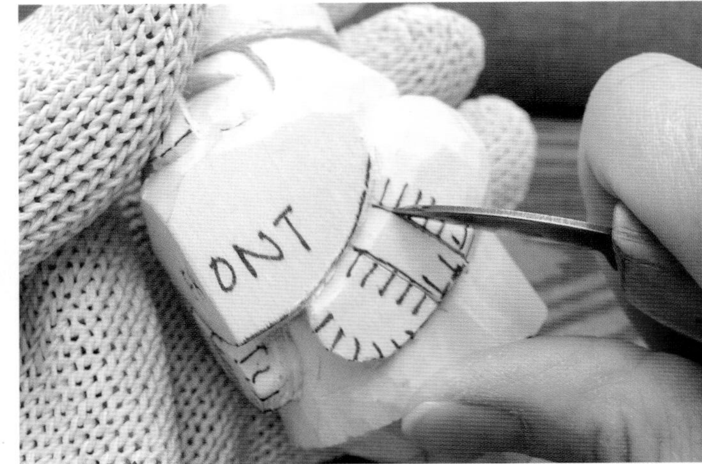
ONT

step 62 Draw in lines to designate the mittens and cuff trim. The mittens are ½ in. long, and the cuff trim is ¼ in. wide.

ONT

step 63 Score these lines and remove a small amount of wood in the shaded areas to define the mittens and cuffs.

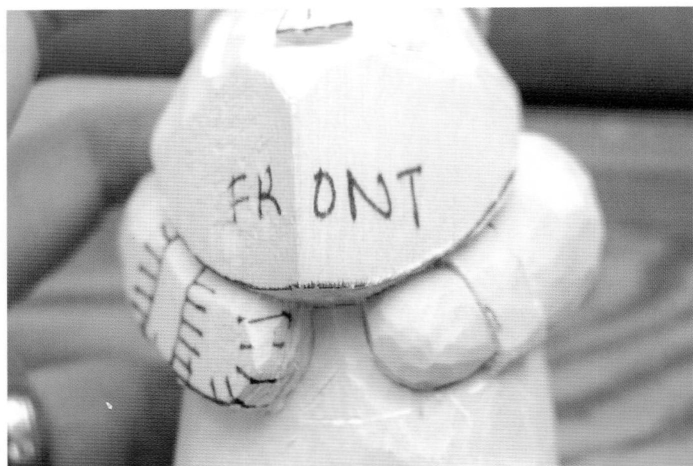
FR ONT

step 64 A comparison shows a shaped mitten and a yet-to-be-shaped mitten.

face details

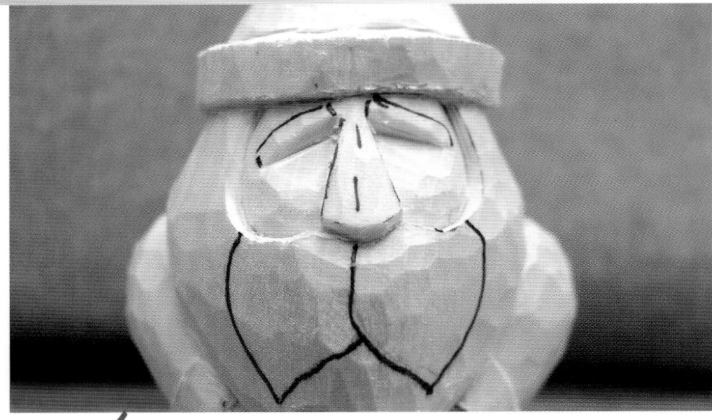

step 65 Draw in the moustache and the eyebrows.

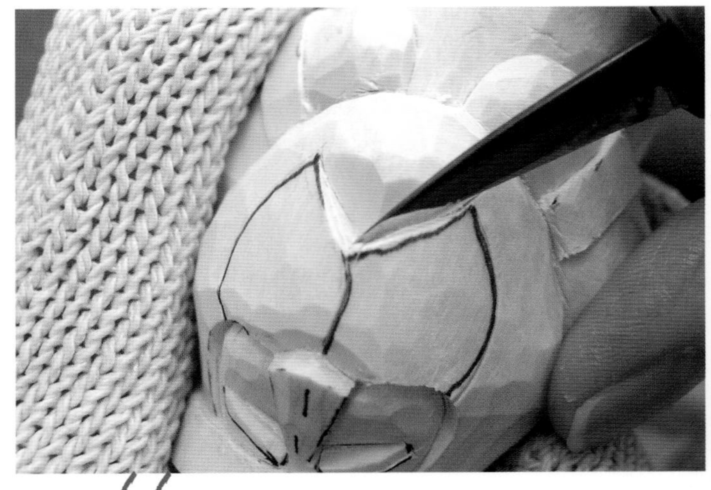

step 66 Score these lines and remove small amounts of wood around the eyebrows and the moustache with a detail knife.

face details

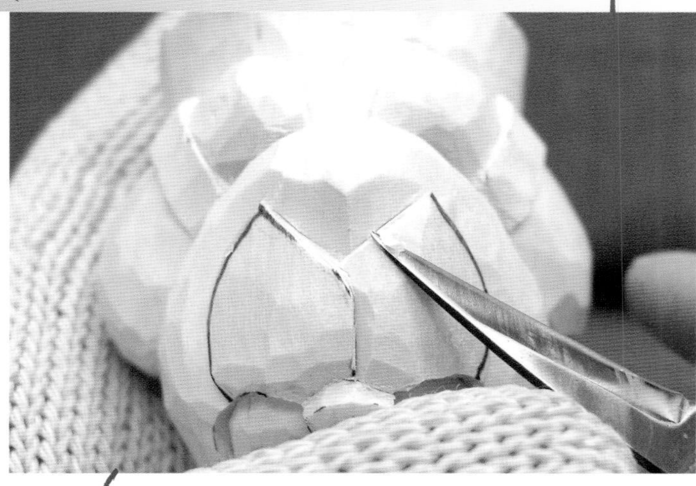

step 67 Round the edges of the moustache.

step 68 Round the sides of the nose.

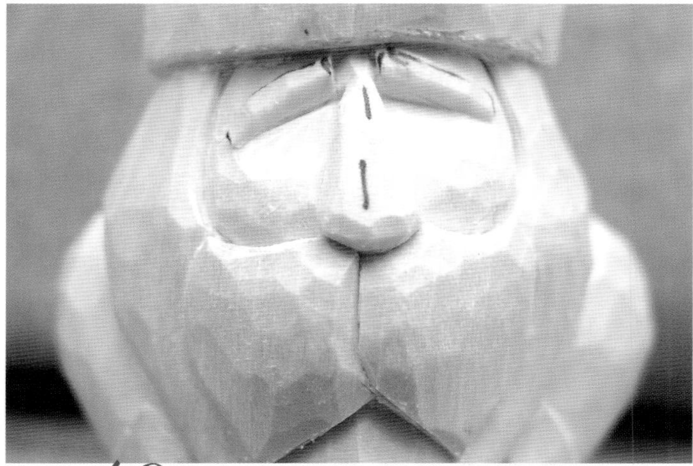

step 69 Round the bottom edge of the beard and the edge of the beard under the cheeks.

coat details

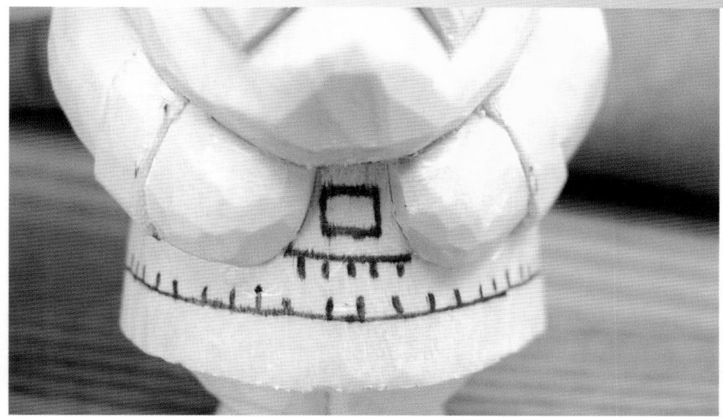

step 70 Draw in the buckle between Santa's mittens. Draw a line ¼ in. up from the bottom of Santa's coat.

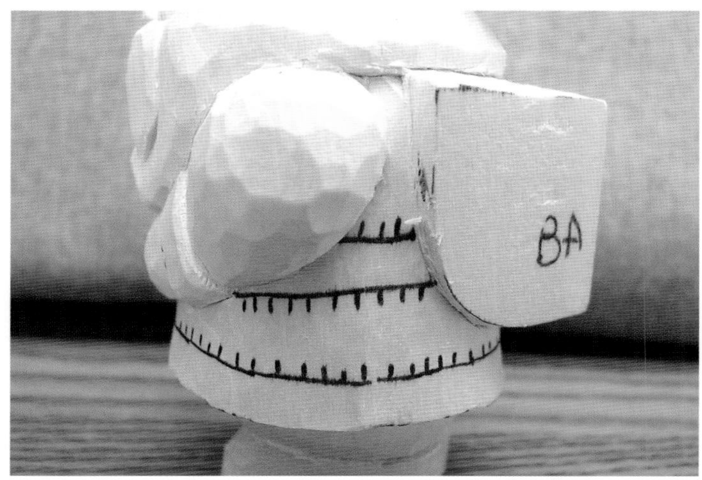
BA

step 71 Draw in the belt on Santa's back on both sides of his pack.

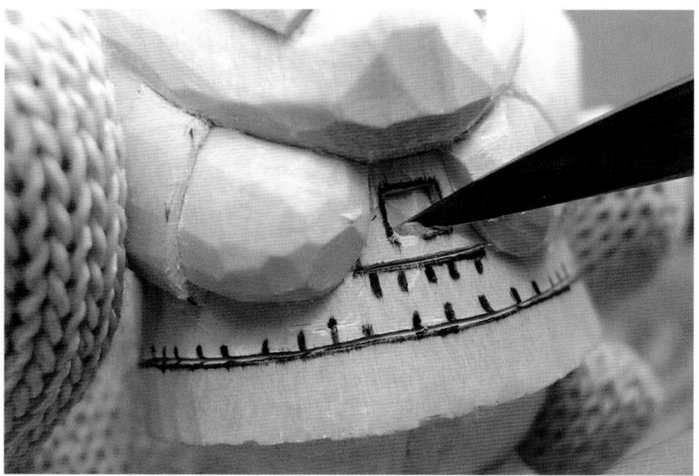

step 72 Carefully remove the wood on the inside square of the belt buckle.

step 73 Score all of these lines and remove wood in the shaded areas to define them.

step 74 Round both edges of the belt and both edges of the bottom trim.

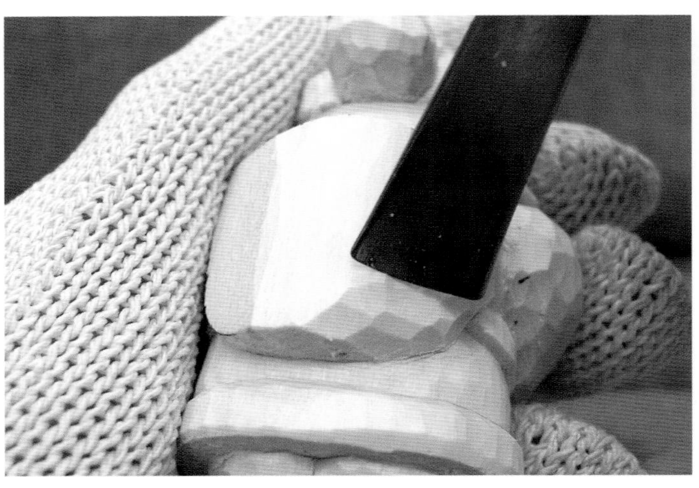

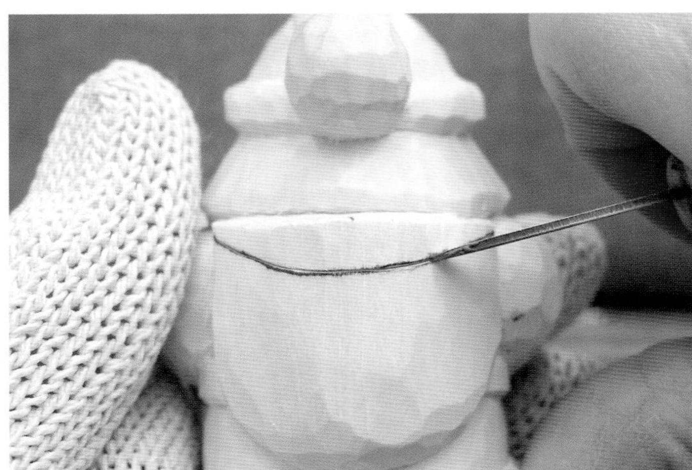

step 75 Using a gouge, round the edge of Santa's pack where they meet his coat.

step 76 Draw a line to designate the top of Santa's pack. Score the line.

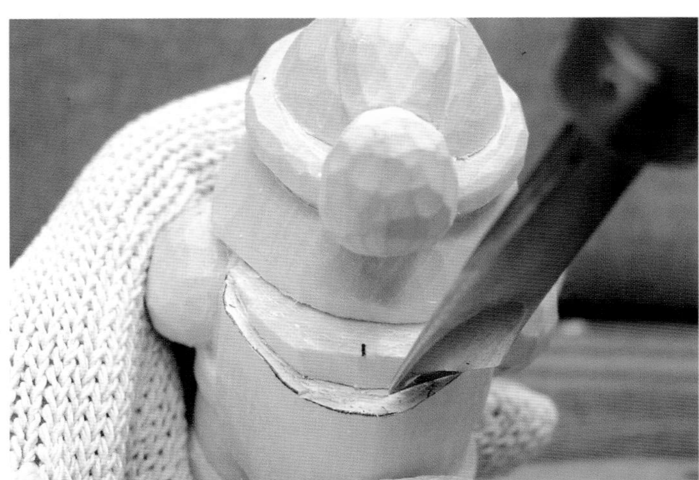

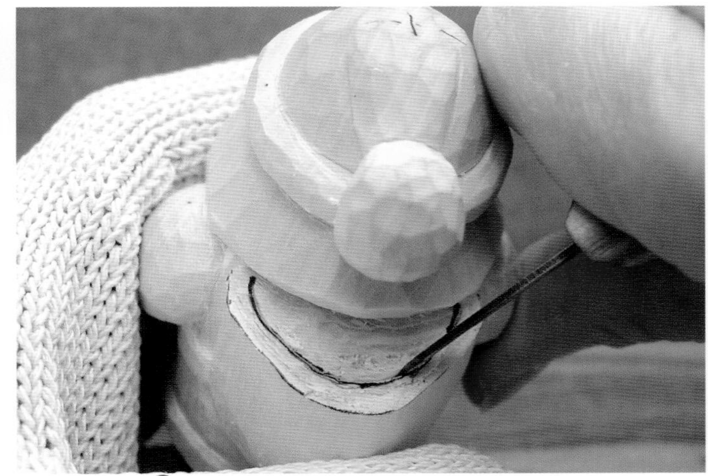

step 77 Remove the wood above the line.

step 78 On top of the pack, draw a line to designate the inside.

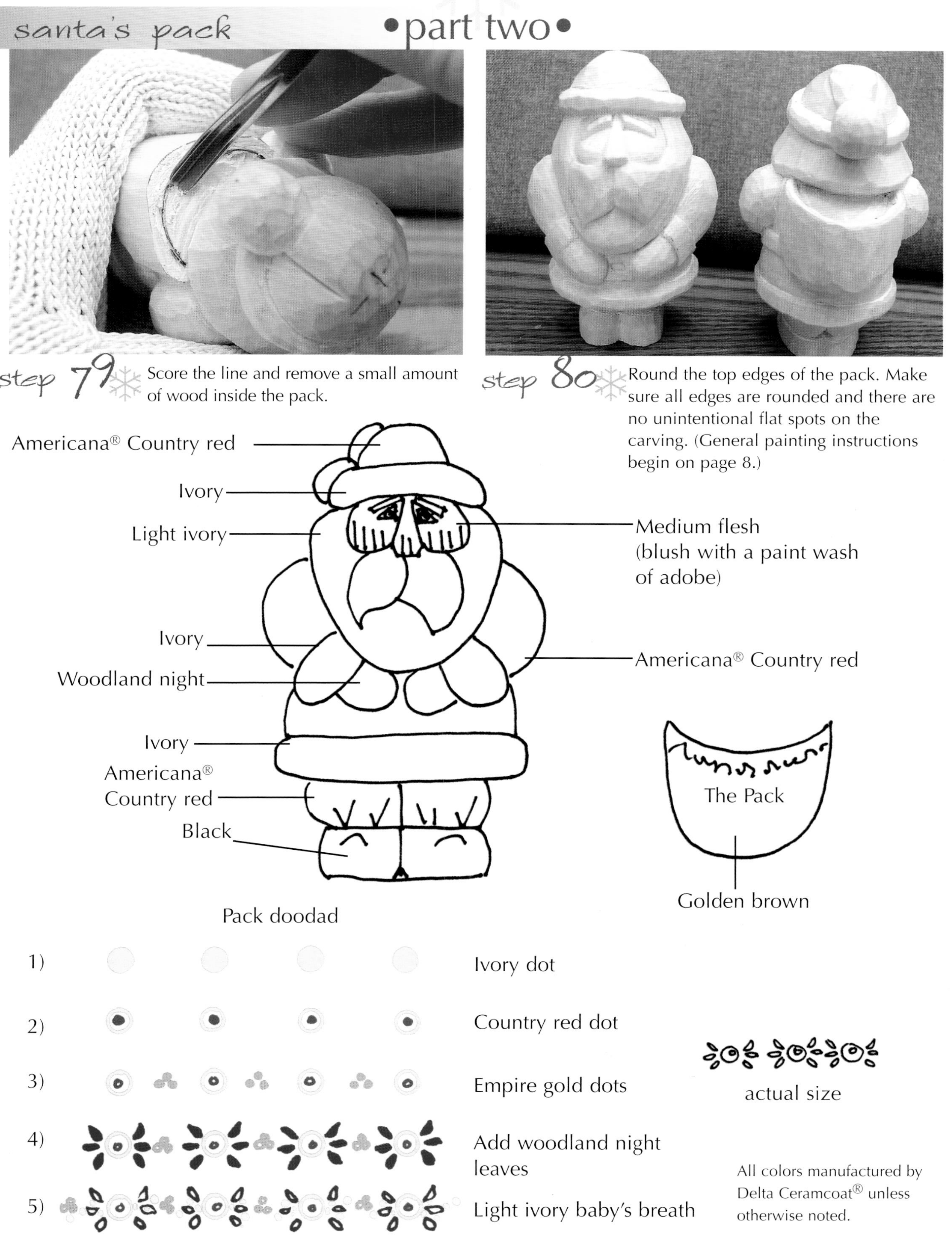
Americana® Country red
Ivory
Light ivory
Medium flesh
(blush with a paint wash
of adobe)
Ivory
Woodland night
Americana® Country red
Ivory
Americana®
Country red
Black
The Pack
Golden brown
Pack doodad
1) Ivory dot
2) Country red dot
3) Empire gold dots
4) Add woodland night leaves
5) Light ivory baby's breath
actual size

step 79 Score the line and remove a small amount of wood inside the pack.

step 80 Round the top edges of the pack. Make sure all edges are rounded and there are no unintentional flat spots on the carving. (General painting instructions begin on page 8.)

All colors manufactured by Delta Ceramcoat® unless otherwise noted.

Weinachtsman Southern Germany

Wood List

Body	1 ea.	3¾" x 2" x 2"
Arm	1 ea.	1" x ¾" x ¾"
Lower Staff	1 ea.	1½" x ¼" x ¼"
Upper Staff	1 ea.	¾" x ¼" x ¼"

Paint List

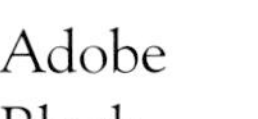

Adobe
Black
Brown iron oxide
Burnt sienna
Americana® Country red
Deep river green
Ivory
Light ivory
Medium flesh
Old parchment
Alpine green
Empire gold

Weinachtsman
Southern Germany

The Pattern

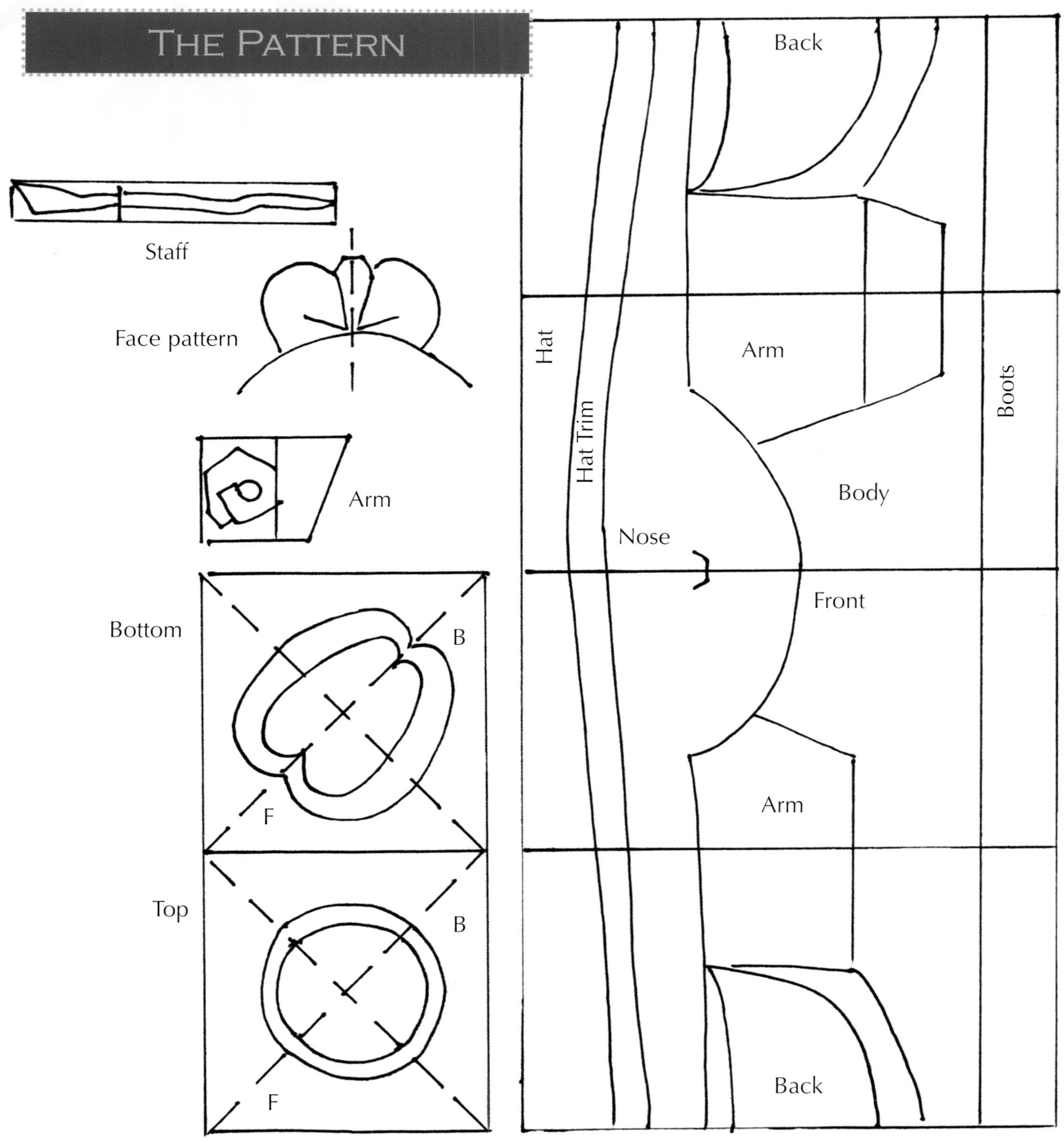
Staff
Face pattern
Arm
Bottom
B
F
Top
B
F
Back
Hat
Hat Trim
Arm
Boots
Body
Nose
Front
Arm
Back

Weinachtsman
Southern Germany

The Color Chart

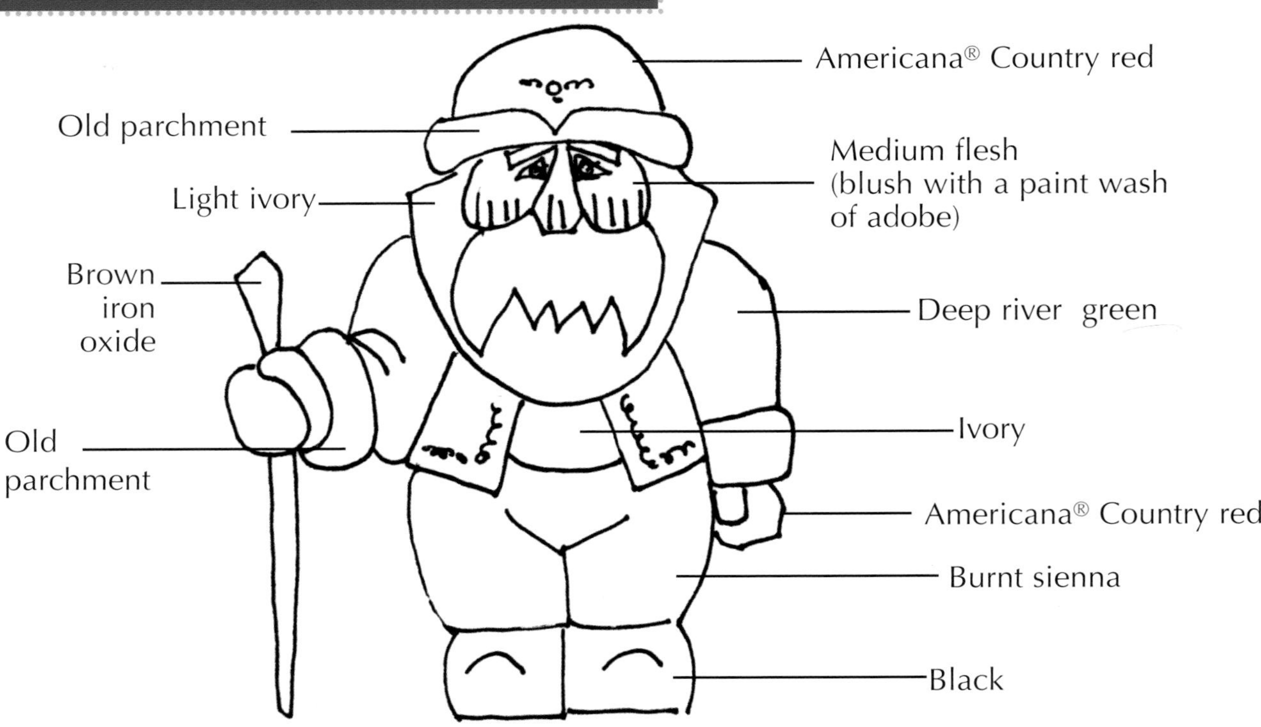
Americana® Country red
Old parchment
Medium flesh
(blush with a paint wash
of adobe)
Light ivory
Brown
iron
oxide
Deep river green
Old
parchment
Ivory
Americana® Country red
Burnt sienna
Black

Coat doodad
1)
Ivory dot
2)
Americana®
Country red dot
3)
Empire gold dot
4)
Add alpine green leaves
5)
Light ivory baby's breath
Actual size
Hat motif

All colors manufactured by Delta Ceramcoat® unless otherwise noted.

Uncle Sam
United States

Wood List		
Body	1 ea.	3¾" x 2" x 2"
Arm	1 ea.	⅞" x ¾" x ¾"
Flag	1 ea.	⅞" x 1¼" x ⅜"
Flag Pole	1 ea.	1½" x ¼" x ¼"

Paint List

Adobe
Brown iron oxide
Americana® Country red
DecoArt® Craft Twinkles Christmas Red
Empire gold
Liberty blue
Light ivory
Medium flesh
Metallic gold
Midnight blue
Prussian blue

Uncle Sam
United States

The Pattern

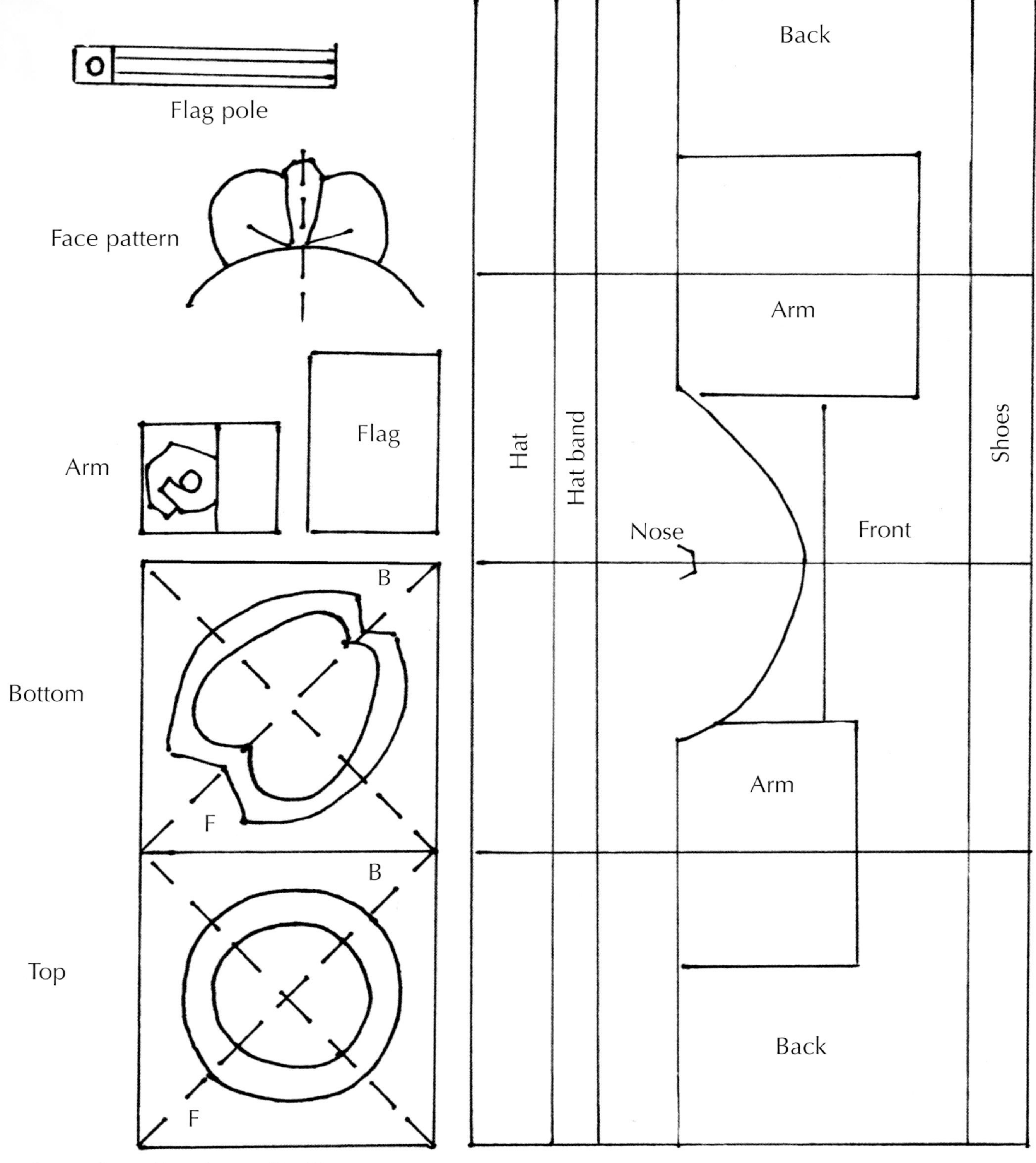
Flag pole
Face pattern
Arm
Flag
Bottom
B
F
Top
B
F
Back
Arm
Hat
Hat band
Nose
Front
Shoes
Arm
Back

Uncle Sam
United States

The Color Chart

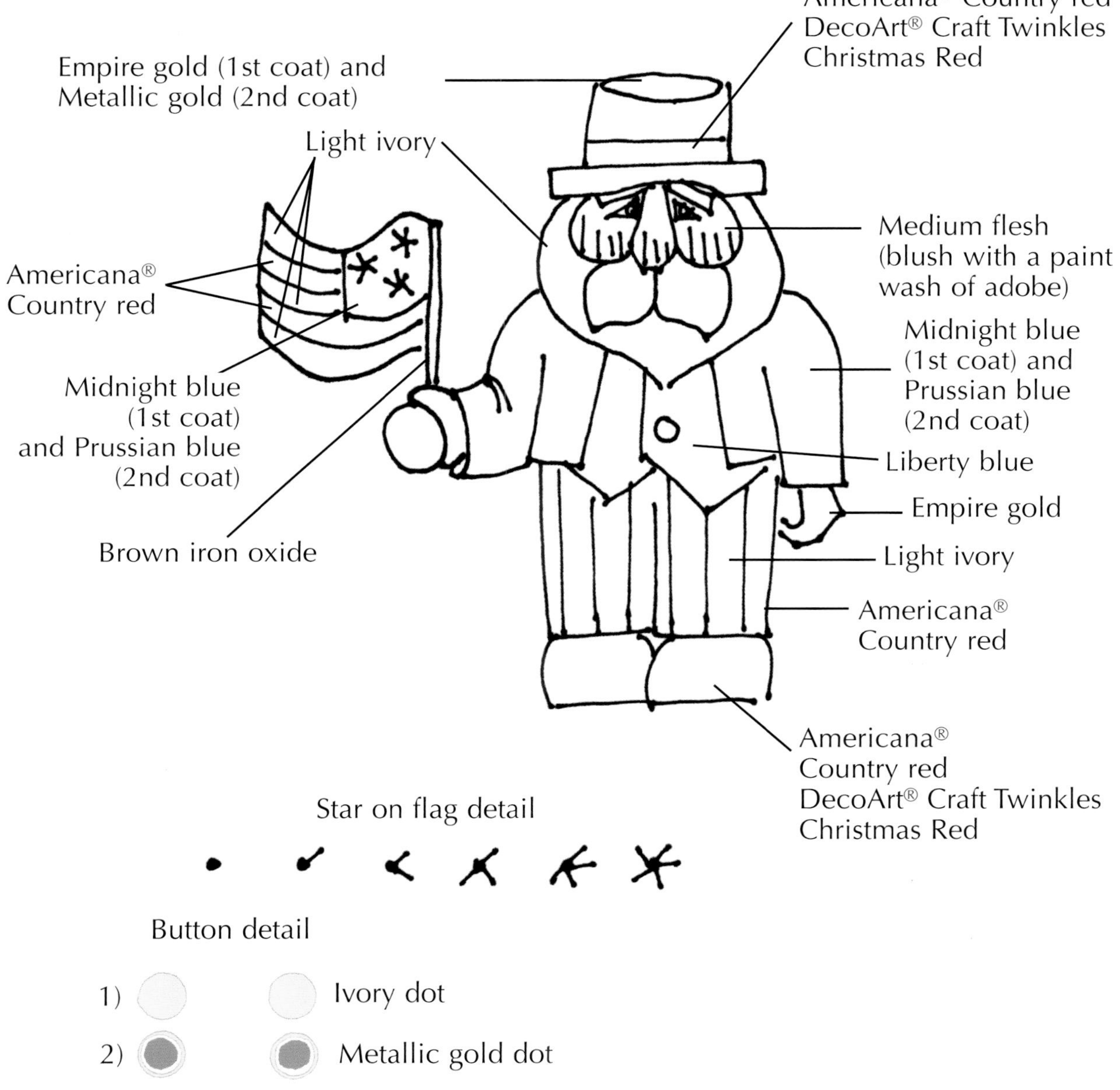
Americana® Country red
DecoArt® Craft Twinkles
Christmas Red
Empire gold (1st coat) and
Metallic gold (2nd coat)
Light ivory
Medium flesh
(blush with a paint
wash of adobe)
Americana®
Country red
Midnight blue
(1st coat) and
Prussian blue
(2nd coat)
Midnight blue
(1st coat)
and Prussian blue
(2nd coat)
Liberty blue
Empire gold
Brown iron oxide
Light ivory
Americana®
Country red
Americana®
Country red
DecoArt® Craft Twinkles
Christmas Red
Star on flag detail
Button detail
1)
Ivory dot
2)
Metallic gold dot

* *

Actual size

All colors manufactured by Delta Ceramcoat® unless otherwise noted.

Sinter Klaas
Netherlands

Wood List

Body	1 ea.	3¾" x 2" x 2"
Arm	2 ea.	1¼" x ¾" x ¾"
Hearts	3 ea.	⅝" x ¾" x ⅜"
Eye Pins	3 ea.	

24 gauge wire to string hearts

Paint List

Adobe
Black
Empire gold
Ivory
Jubilee green
Light Ivory
Medium flesh
Purple
Americana® Country red

Sinter Klaas
Netherlands

The Pattern

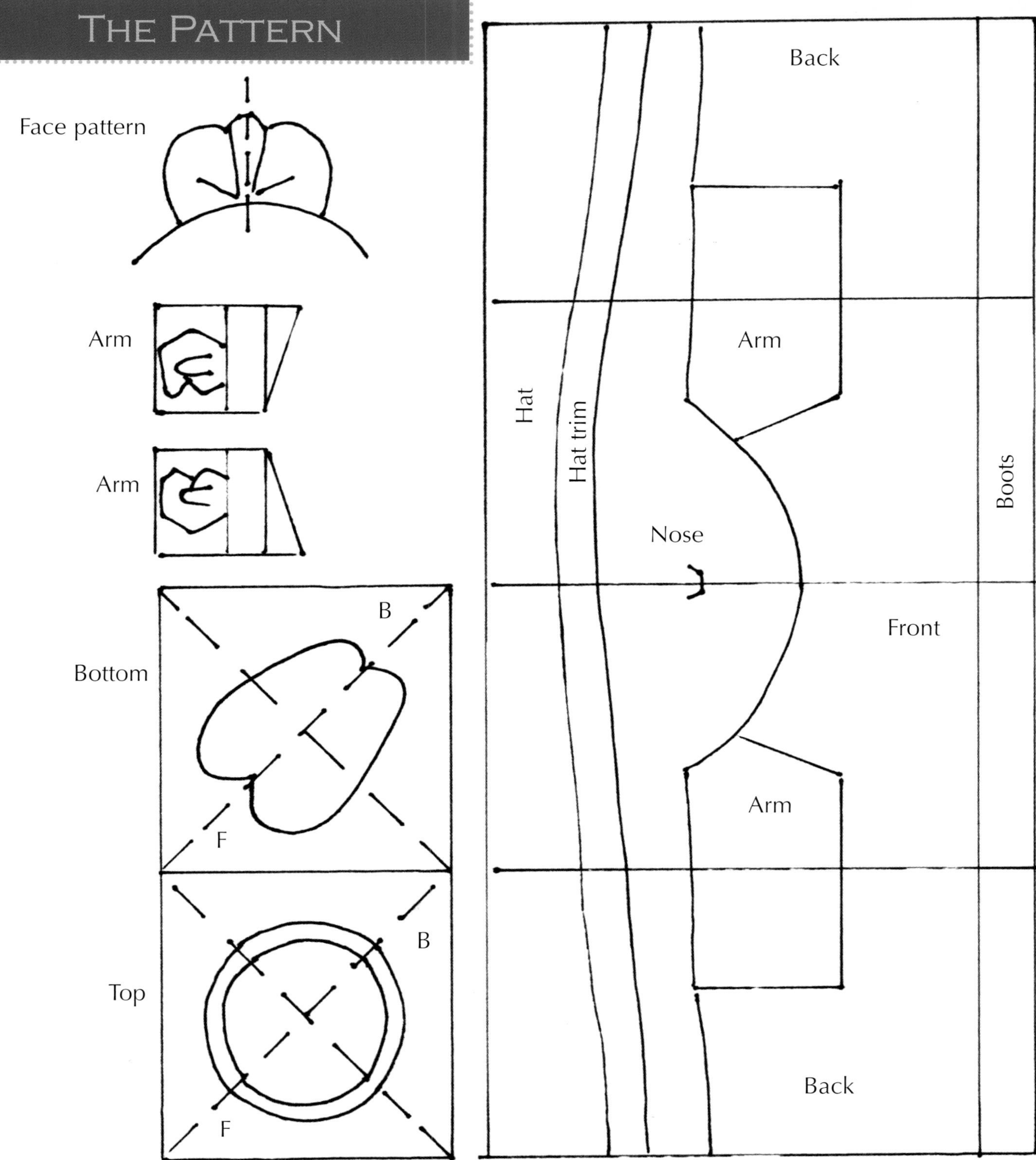
Face pattern
Arm
Arm
Bottom
B
F
Top
B
F
Back
Arm
Hat
Hat trim
Nose
Boots
Front
Arm
Back

Sinter Klaas Netherlands

The Color Chart

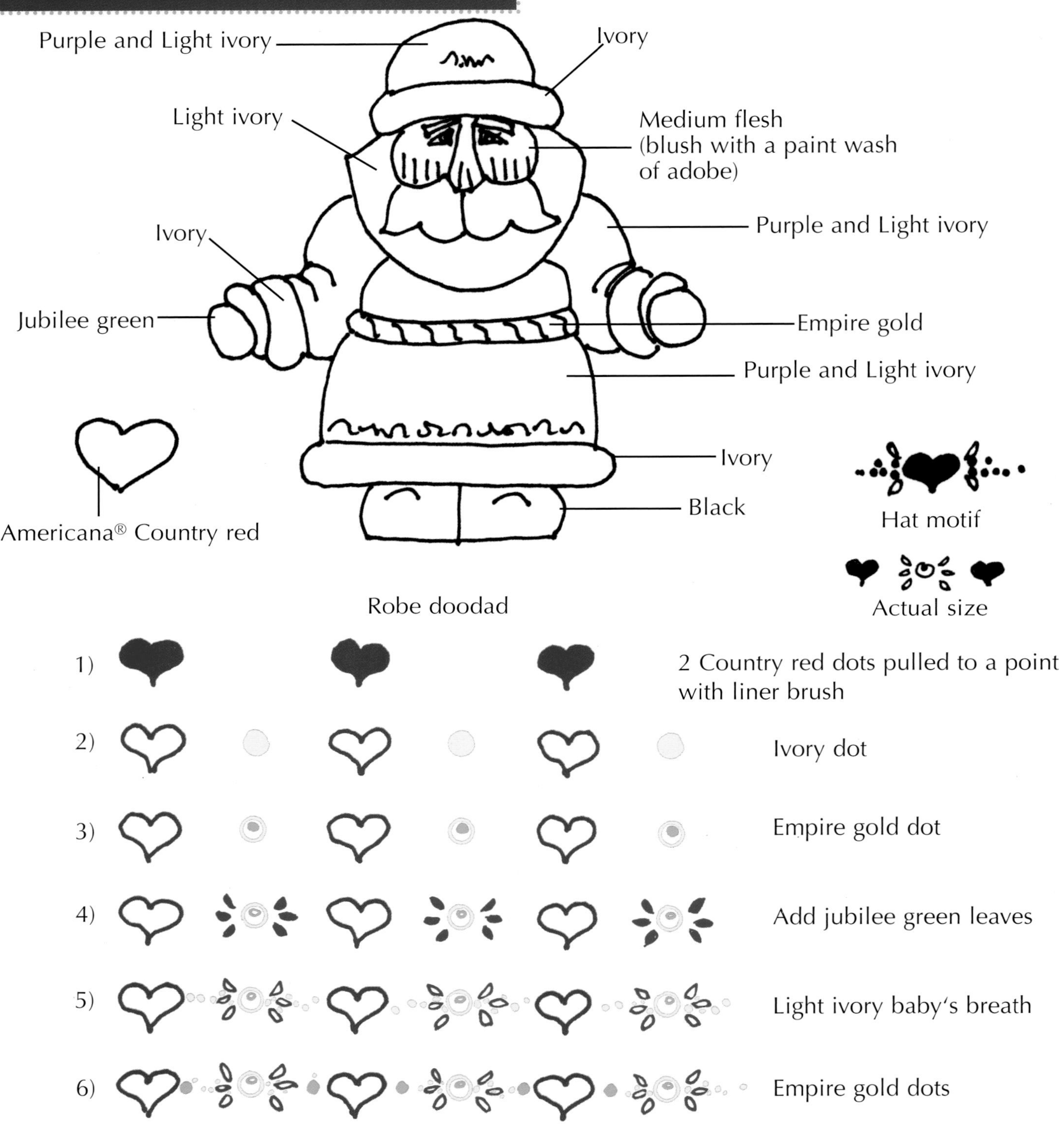
Purple and Light ivory
Ivory
Light ivory
Medium flesh
(blush with a paint wash
of adobe)
Ivory
Purple and Light ivory
Jubilee green
Empire gold
Purple and Light ivory
Ivory
Black
Americana® Country red
Hat motif
Actual size
Robe doodad
1) 2 Country red dots pulled to a point with liner brush
2) Ivory dot
3) Empire gold dot
4) Add jubilee green leaves
5) Light ivory baby's breath
6) Empire gold dots

All colors manufactured by Delta Ceramcoat® unless otherwise noted.

Niklo
Austria

The Pattern

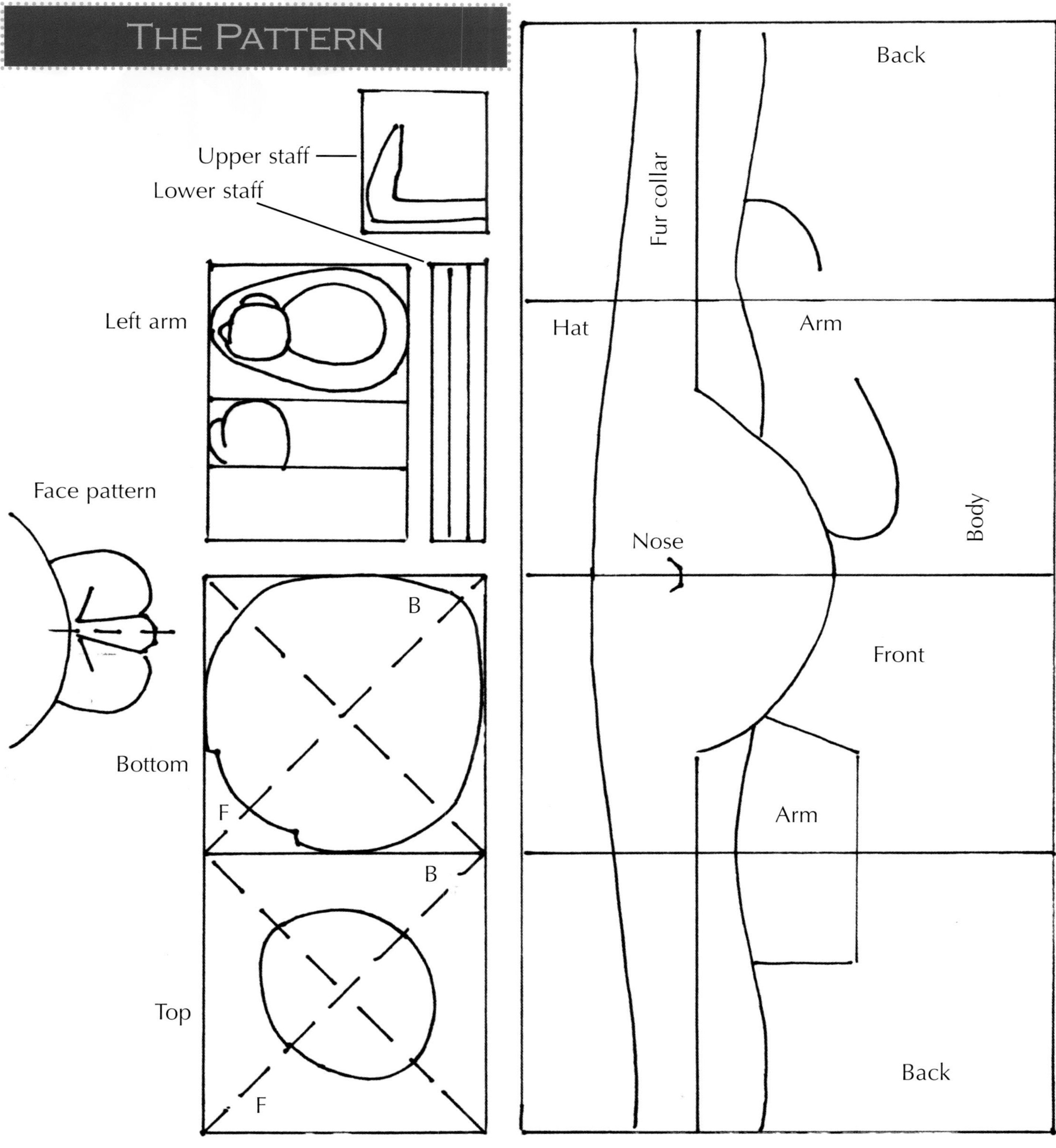
Upper staff
Lower staff
Left arm
Face pattern
Bottom
B
F
B
Top
F
Back
Fur collar
Hat
Arm
Nose
Body
Front
Arm
Back

Niklo
Austria

The Color Chart

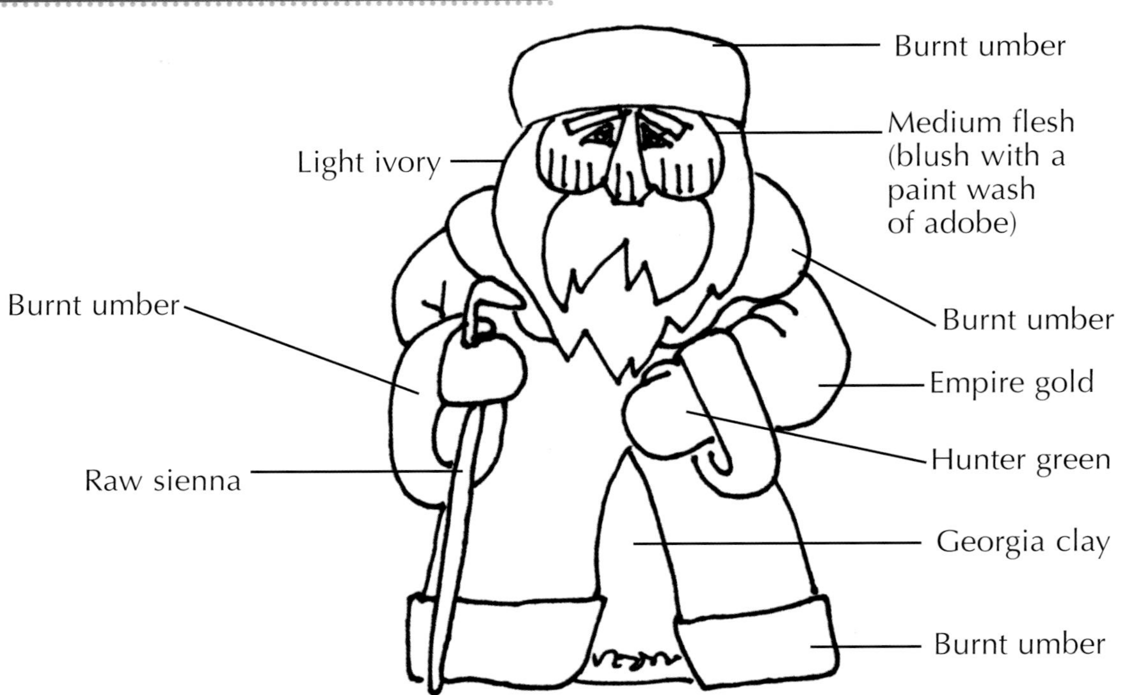
Burnt umber
Medium flesh (blush with a paint wash of adobe)
Light ivory
Burnt umber
Burnt umber
Empire gold
Hunter green
Raw sienna
Georgia clay
Burnt umber

Inner robe doodad

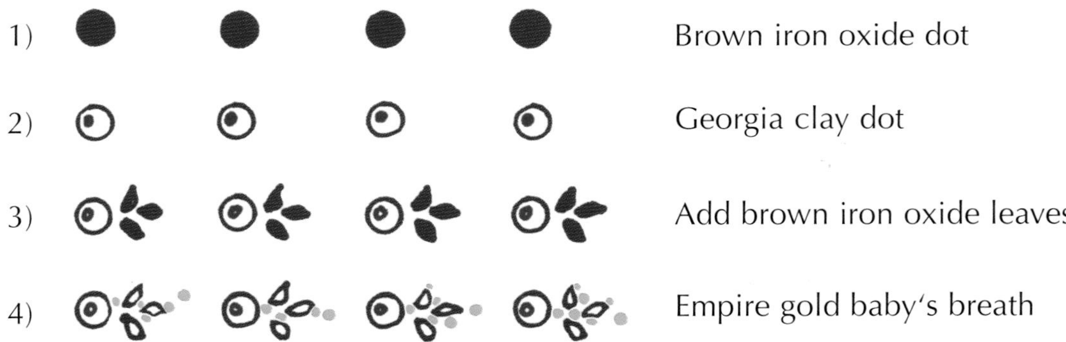
1)
2)
3)
4)
Brown iron oxide dot
Georgia clay dot
Add brown iron oxide leaves
Empire gold baby's breath

Actual size

All colors manufactured by Delta Ceramcoat® unless otherwise noted.

Hospodar
Ukraine

Wood List

Body	1 ea.	3¾" x 2" x 2"
Arm	1 ea.	1" x ¾" x ¾"
Tree	1 ea.	1¼" x ¾" x ¾"

Paint List

Adobe
Black
Brown iron oxide
Chrome green light
Empire gold
Hunter green
Light ivory
Maple sugar brown
Medium flesh
Americana® Napa red
Pine green

Hospodar
Ukraine

The Pattern

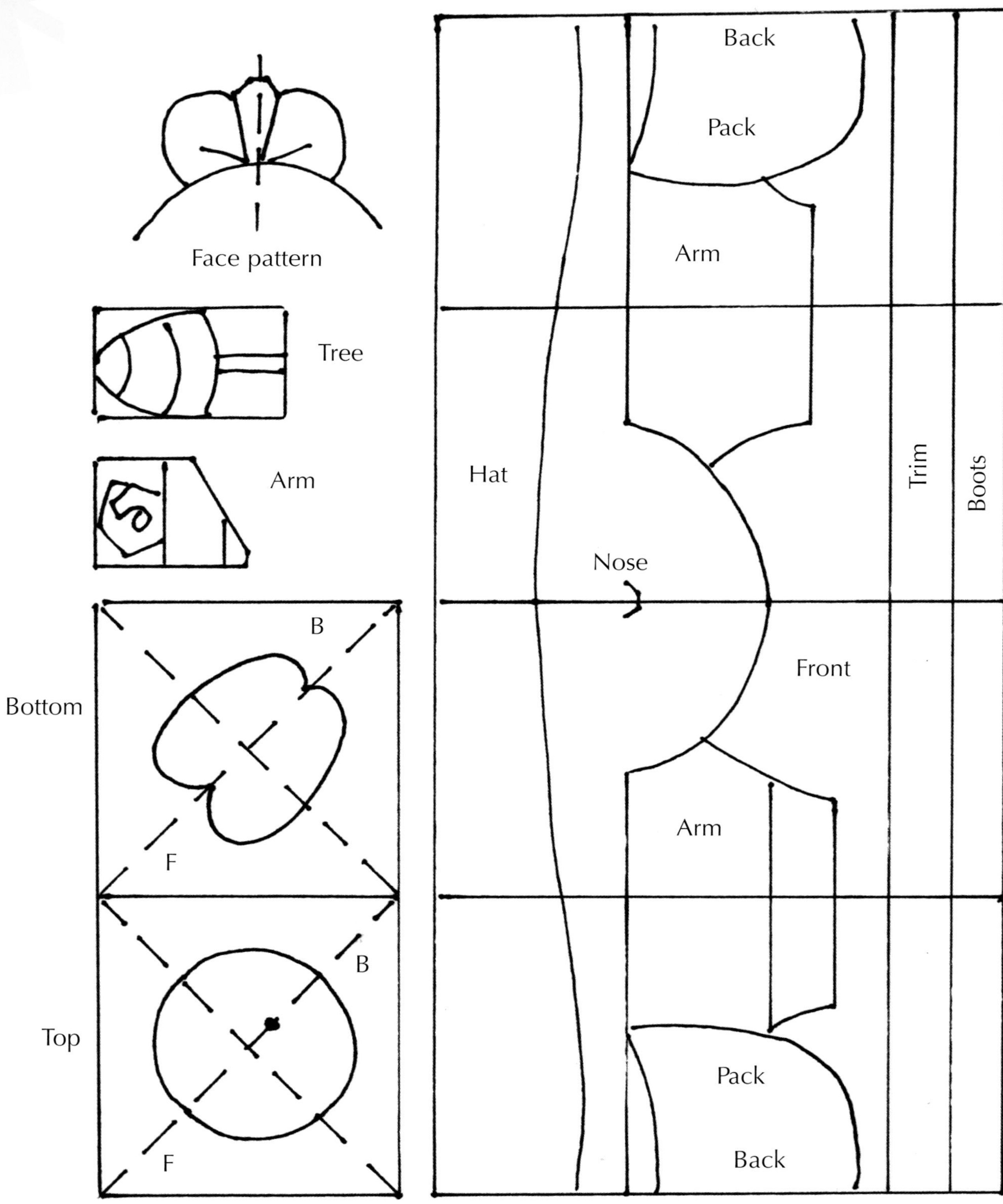
Face pattern
Tree
Arm
Bottom
B
F
Top
B
F
Hat
Back
Pack
Arm
Nose
Front
Arm
Pack
Back
Trim
Boots

•part two•

Hospodar
Ukraine

The Color Chart

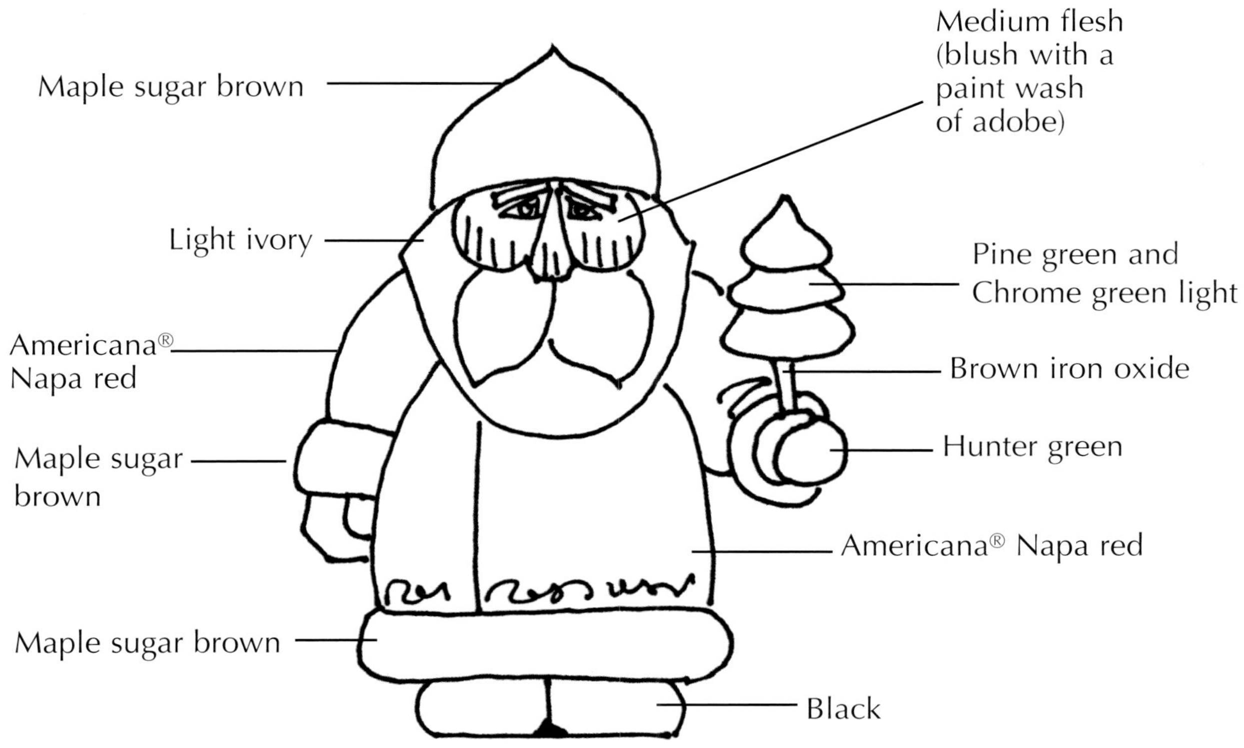
Maple sugar brown
Medium flesh (blush with a paint wash of adobe)
Light ivory
Pine green and Chrome green light
Americana® Napa red
Brown iron oxide
Maple sugar brown
Hunter green
Americana® Napa red
Maple sugar brown
Black

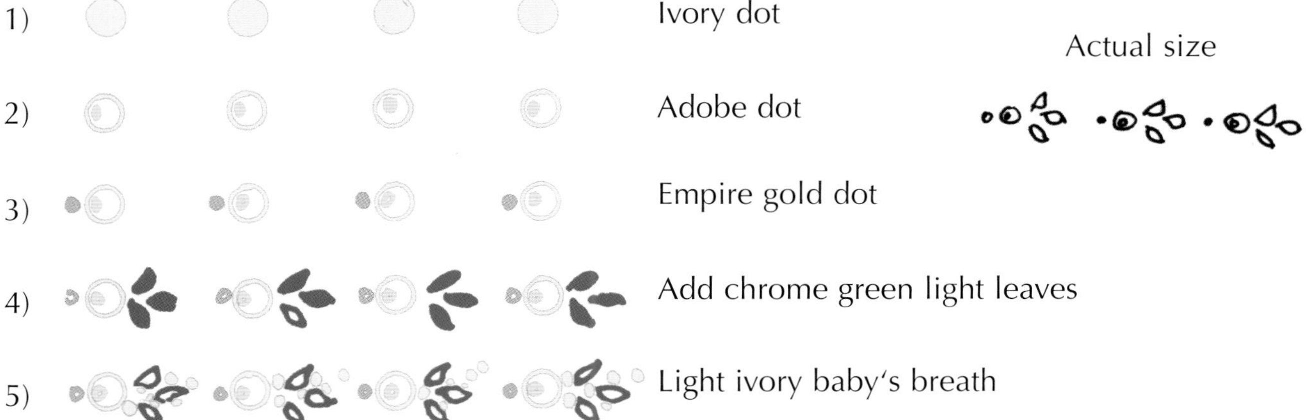
Robe doodad
1) Ivory dot
2) Adobe dot
3) Empire gold dot
4) Add chrome green light leaves
5) Light ivory baby's breath
Actual size

All colors manufactured by Delta Ceramcoat® unless otherwise noted.

Cosmic Santa
Out of this World

Wood List

Body 1 ea. 3¾" x 2" x 2"

Paint List

Adobe
Americana® Country red
Empire gold
Jubilee green
Light Ivory
Medium flesh
Metallic gold
Purple

Cosmic Santa
Out of this World

The Pattern

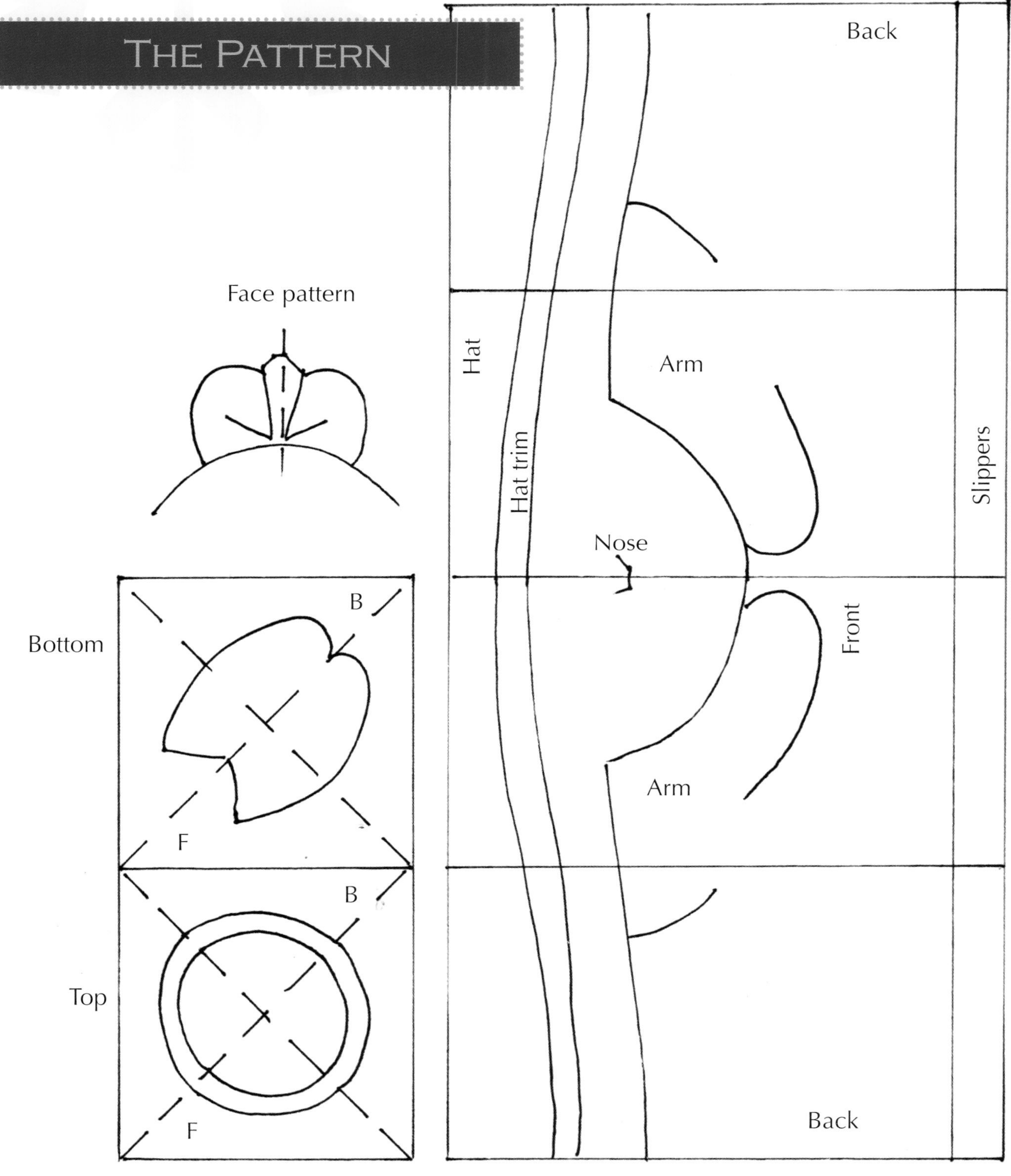
Back
Face pattern
Hat
Hat trim
Arm
Slippers
Nose
Bottom
B
F
Front
Arm
B
Top
F
Back

Cosmic Santa
Out of this World

The Color Chart

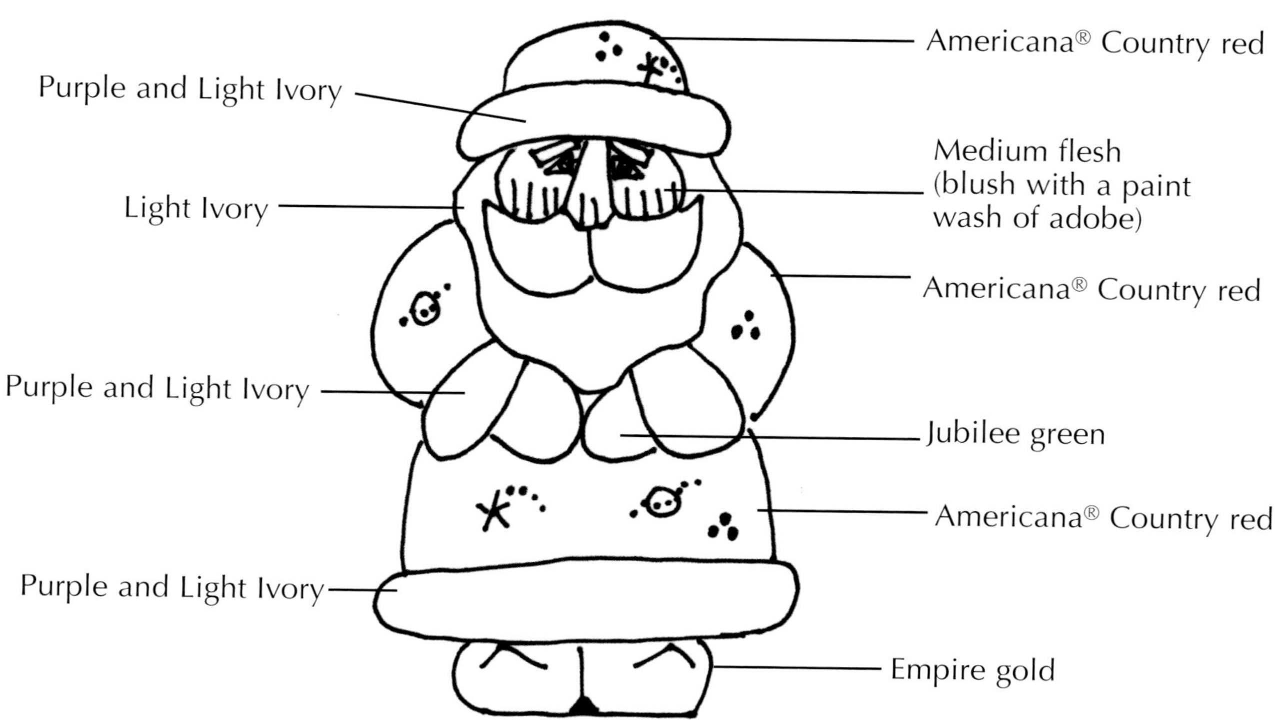
Americana® Country red
Purple and Light Ivory
Medium flesh
(blush with a paint
wash of adobe)
Light Ivory
Americana® Country red
Purple and Light Ivory
Jubilee green
Americana® Country red
Purple and Light Ivory
Empire gold

Robe and hat doodads

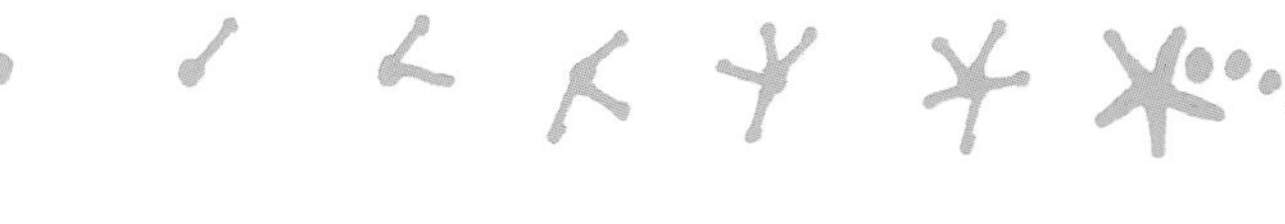

Descending metallic gold dots
Metallic gold dot, pull out color from dot for each ray of star

Purple and Light Ivory dot

Light Ivory wavy dot line

Jubilee green

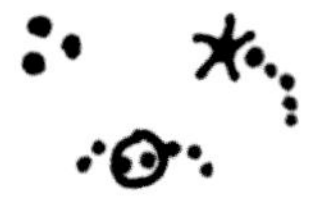

Actual size

All colors manufactured by Delta Ceramcoat® unless otherwise noted.

Carving & Painting Shelf-Sitting Santas

part three

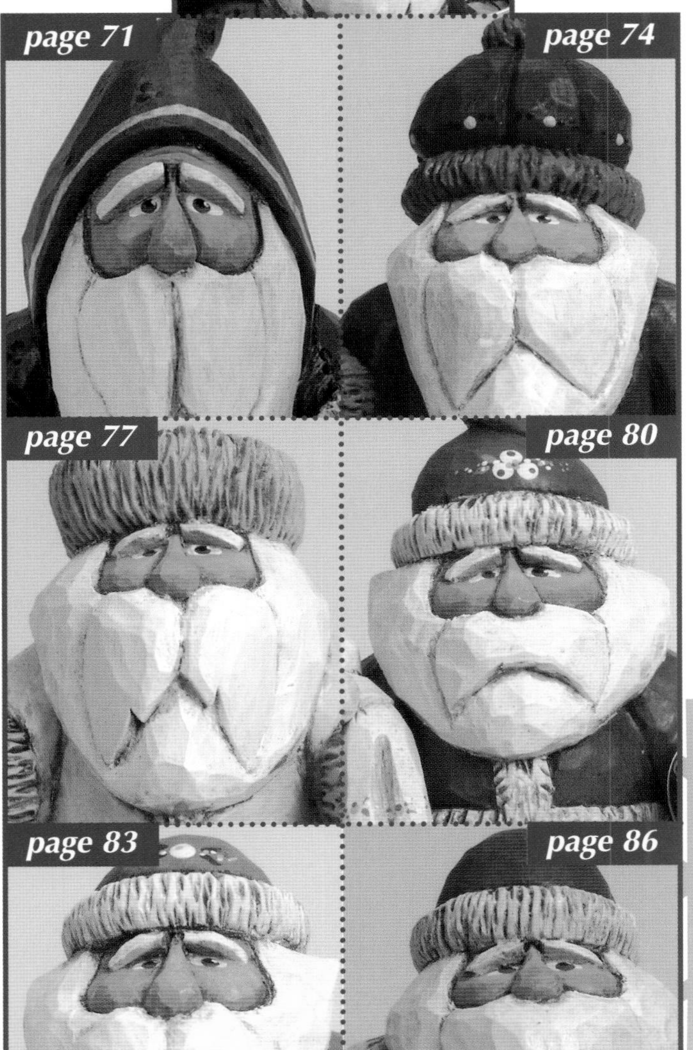
page 50
page 71
page 74
page 77
page 80
page 83
page 86

Shelf-sitting Santas are designed to sit firmly on the edge of a shelf, desk, or computer, with their feet dangling over the side. They are a bit more challenging than the standing Santas in the beginning of this book—but only because they require you to carve and assemble some small parts. The same basic carving cuts and painting techniques are used when creating these shelf-sitting Santas.

Father Christmas England

Wood List

Body	1 ea.	3" x 2" x 2"
Arms	2 ea.	1½" x ¾" x ¾"
Boots	2 ea.	¾" x 1" x ⅝"
Skirt	1 ea.	⅞" x 2" x ¾"
	1 ea.	⅞" x 3" x ¾"
Apples	3 ea.	⅝" x ⅝" x ⅝"
Eye Pins	4 ea.	
Apple Stems	3 ea.	sandwich picks
24 gauge wire		

Paint List

Adobe
Black
Brown iron oxide
Chrome green light
Empire gold
Hunter green
Light ivory
Medium flesh
Pine green
Red iron oxide

Father Christmas England

The Pattern

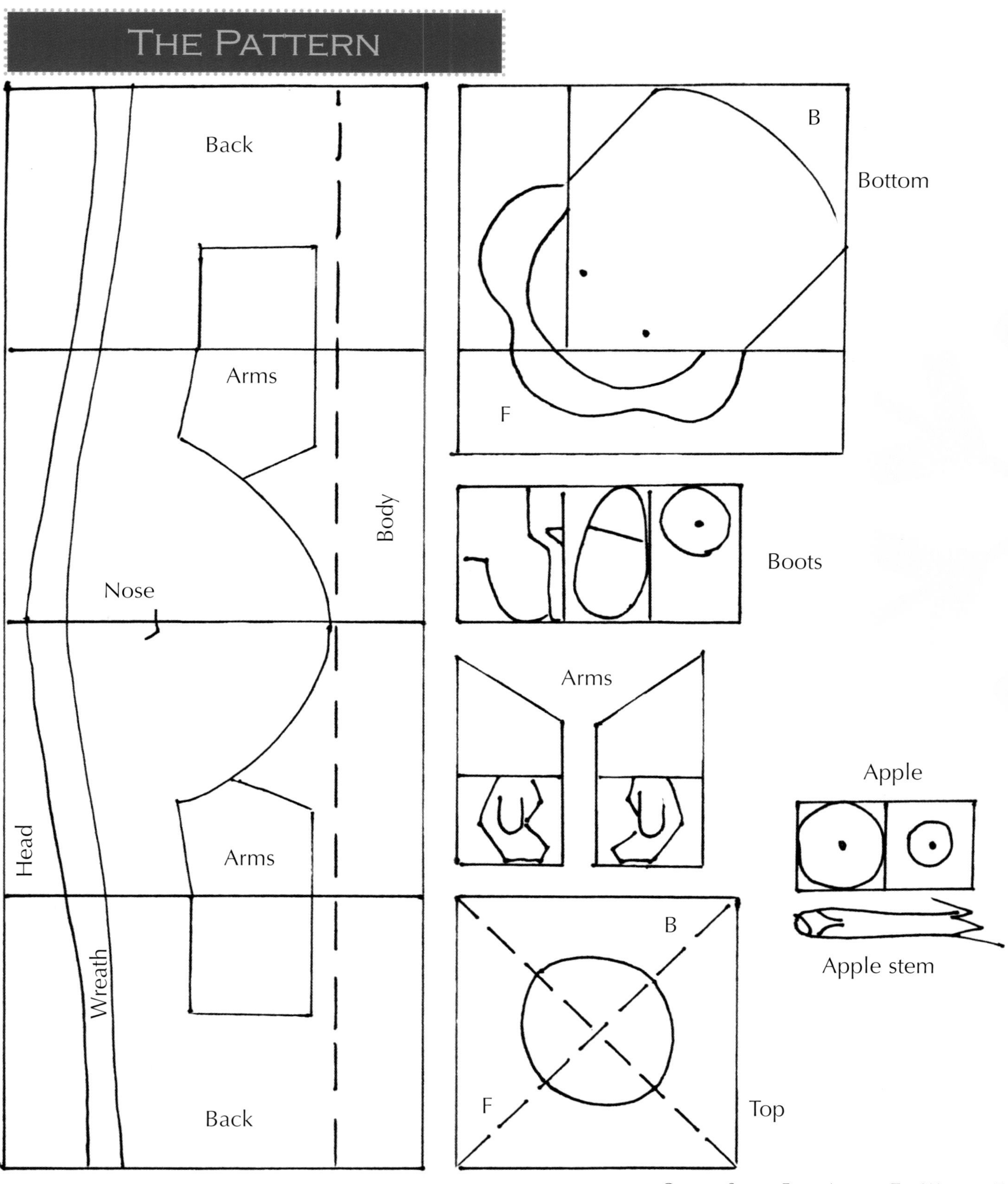
Back
Arms
Body
Nose
Head
Arms
Wreath
Back
B
Bottom
F
Boots
Arms
Apple
B
Apple stem
F
Top

•part three•

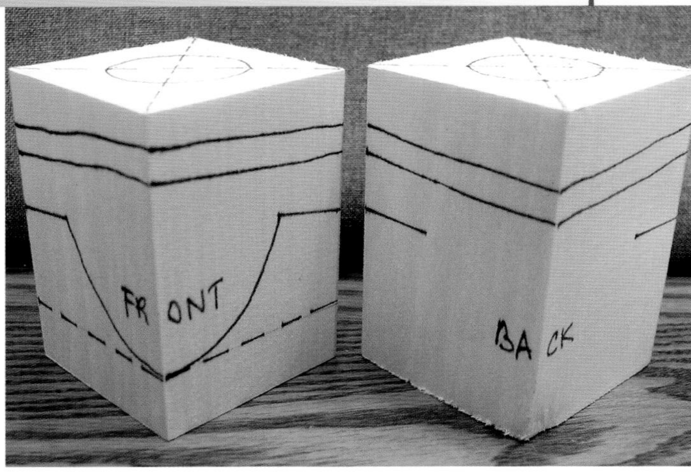
FRONT
BACK

step 1 Transfer the pattern for Father Christmas to the sides, top and bottom of the wood block.

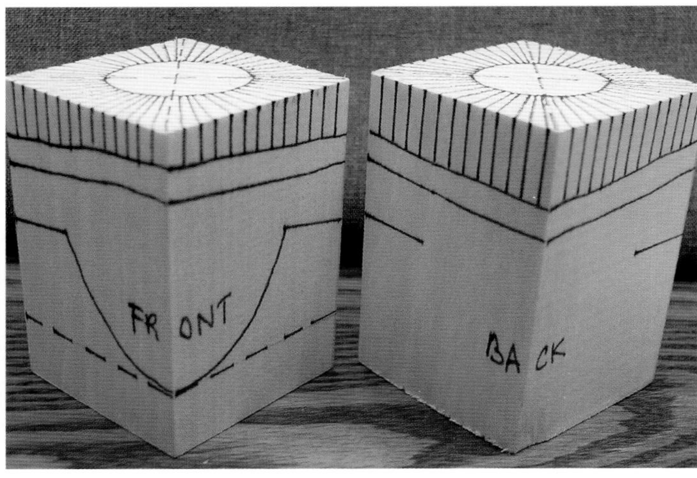
FRONT
BACK

step 2 Your first step will be to remove the wood in the shaded head area.

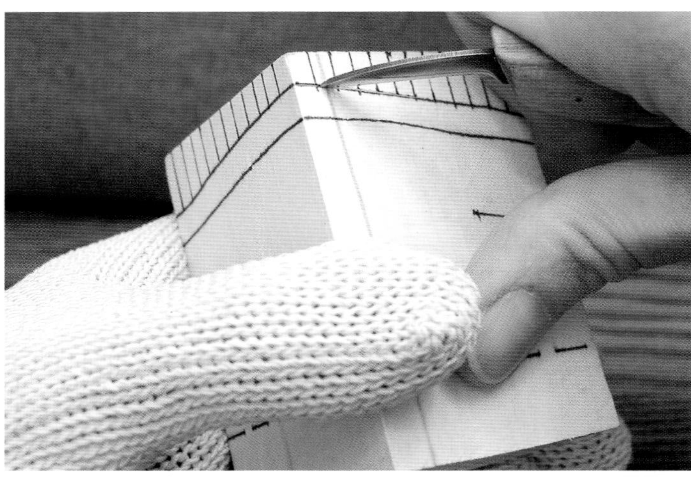

step 3 Score the line directly under the shaded area.

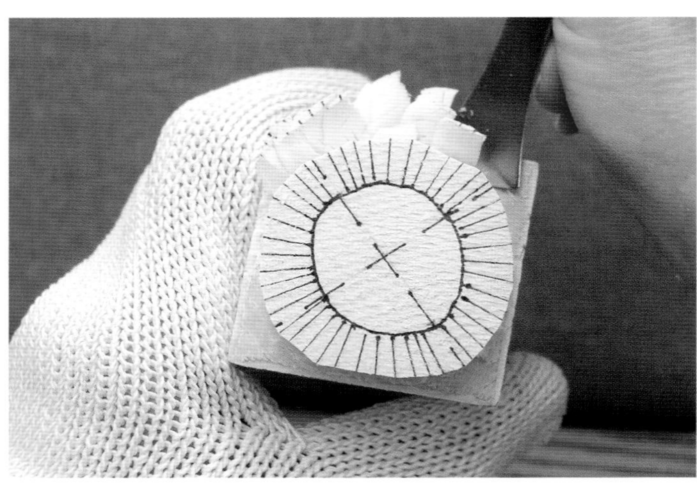

step 4 Remove the wood to the pattern line on the top of the block.

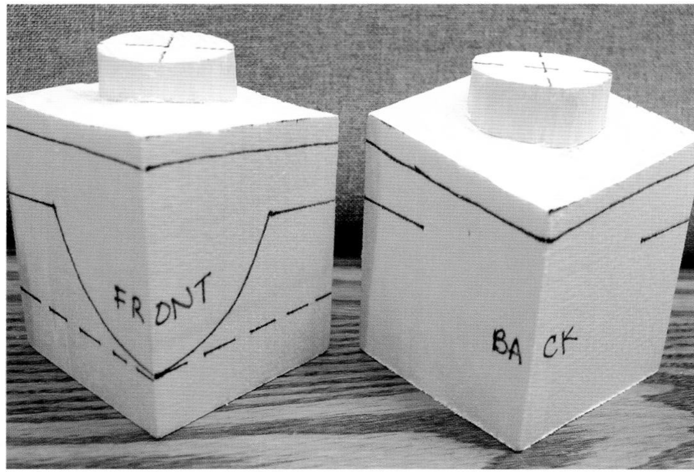
FRONT
BACK

step 5 Your block will look like this, front and back.

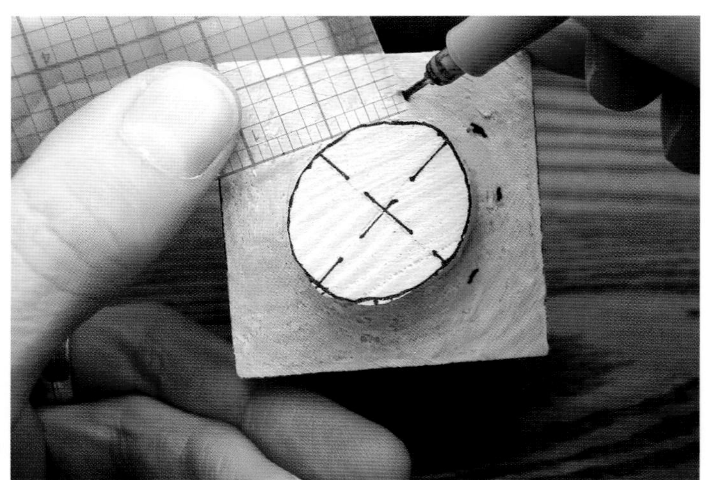

step 6 Next, measure ⅛ in. out from the base of the head in several places.

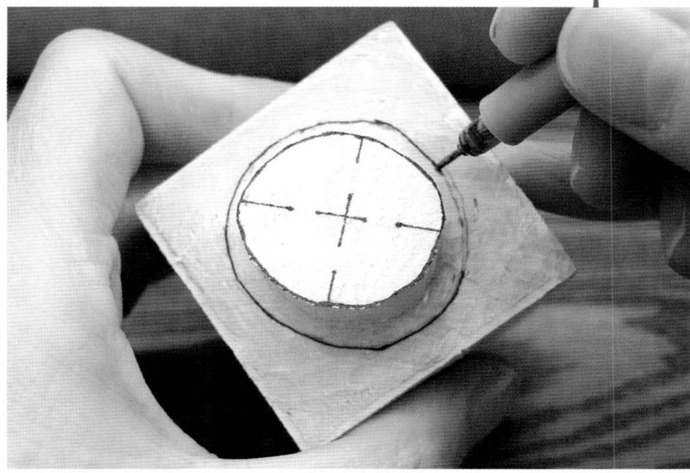

step 7 Connect the marks to form a circle ⅛ in. wider than the base of the head.

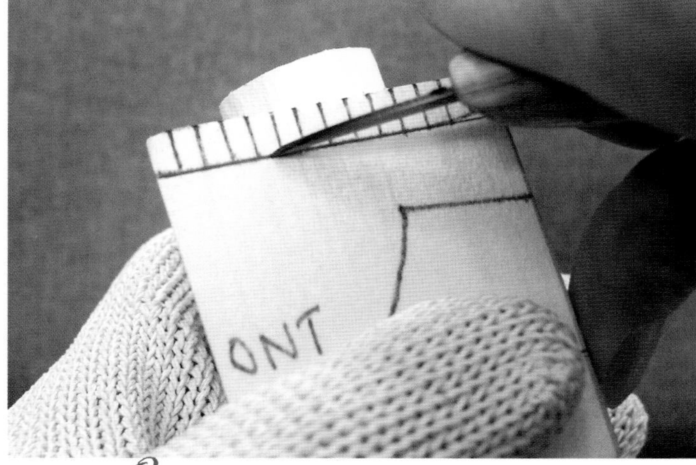
ONT

step 8 Score the line directly beneath the shaded area.

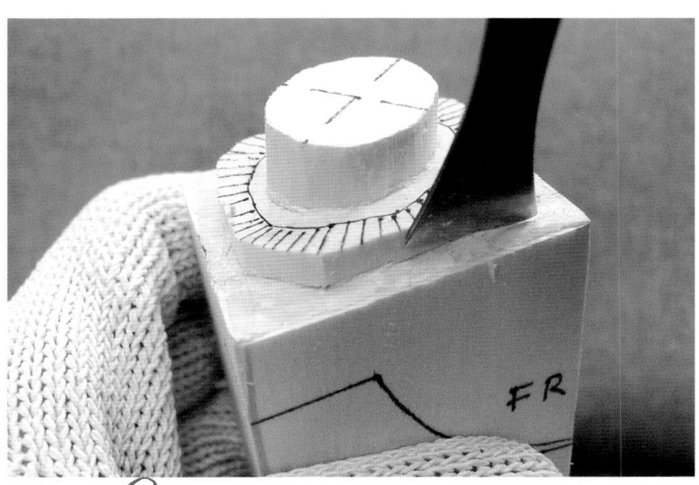
FR

step 9 Remove the wood to the circle just drawn.

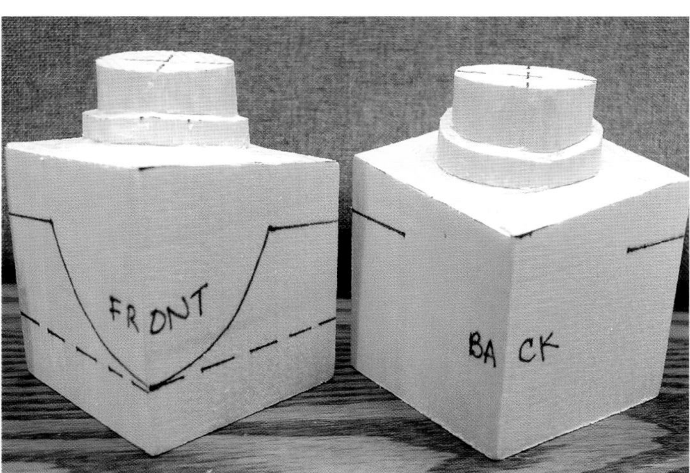
FRONT
BACK

step 10 This will become the wreath around Father Christmas' head.

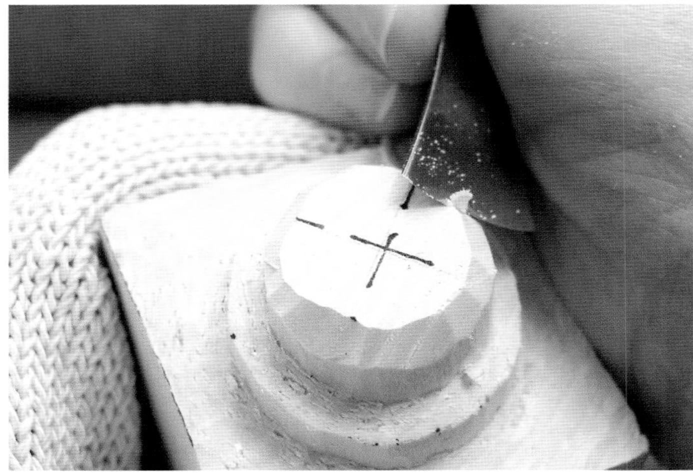

step 11 Round the top of the head with the gouge.

step 12 Next use the detail knife to further shape the head.

Father's shoulders

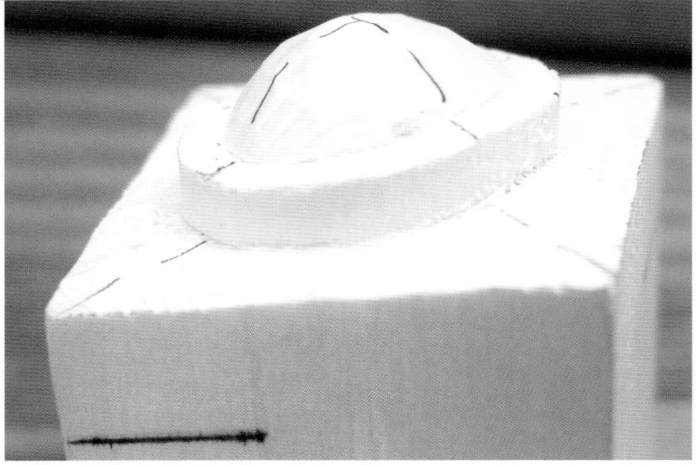

step 13 The progress so far.

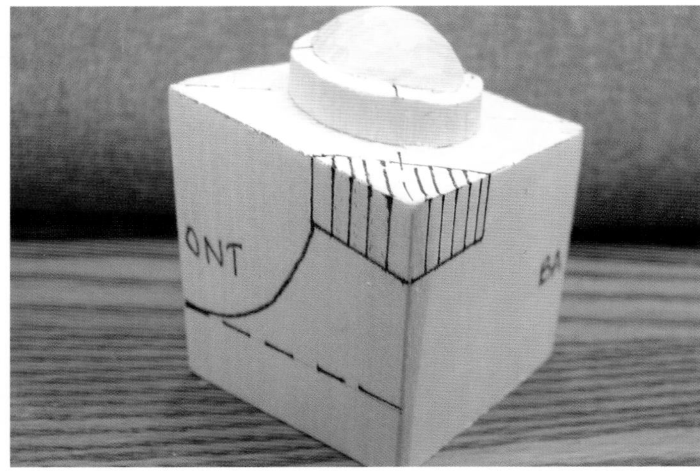
ONT
BA

step 14 Wood will be removed from this shaded area next.

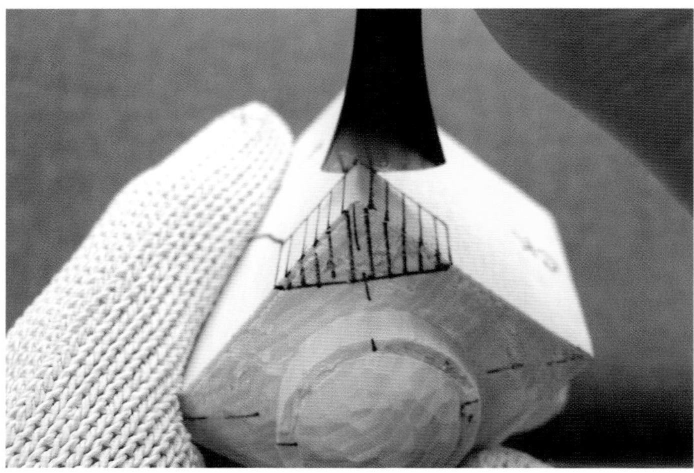

step 15 Push the gouge into the line above the shoulder to create a stop cut.

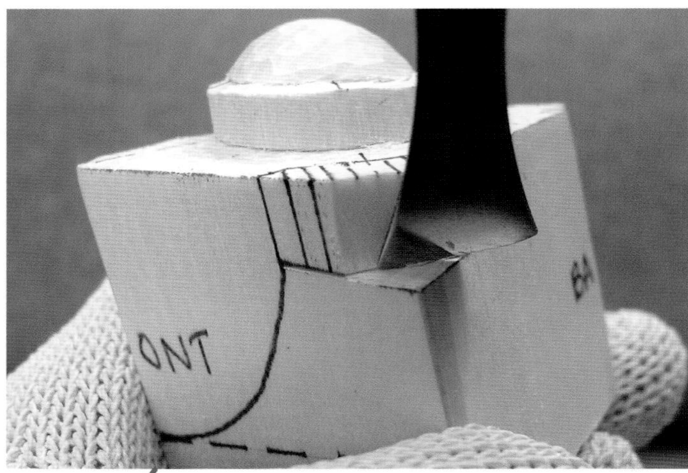
ONT
BA

step 16 Then turn the wood around and carve back down to the stop cut.

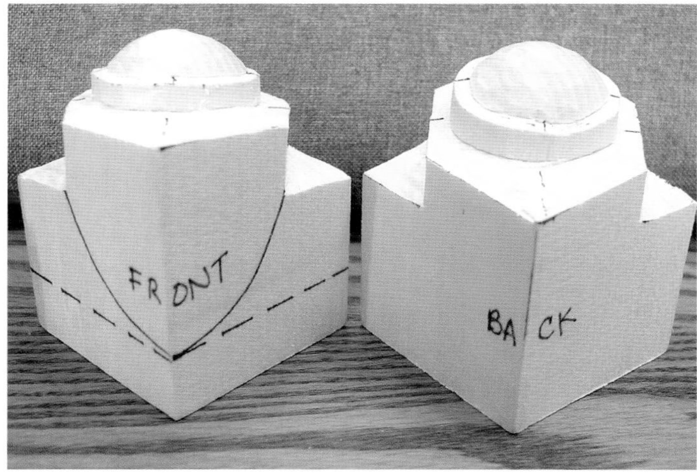
FRONT
BACK

step 17 Repeat this step on the opposite side of the blank so the wood above both shoulders is removed.

Father's face

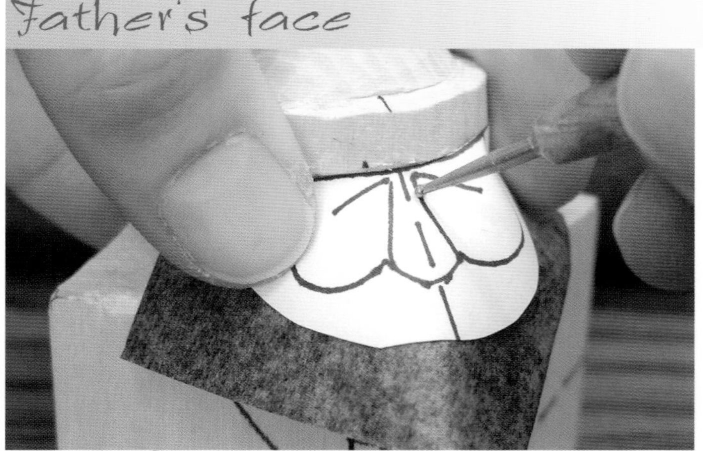

step 18 The faces of the Santas are carved with the same techniques. Trace the face pattern below the wreath and continue to carve the face, referring to the directions on pages 18-19.

•part three•

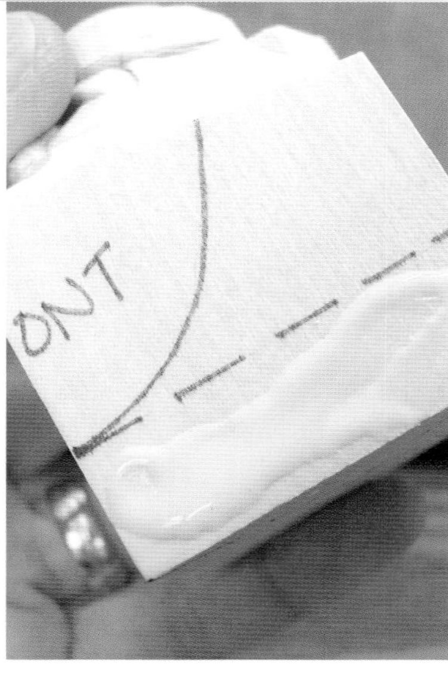
ONT

step 19

Using Carpenter's wood glue, attach the ⅞" x 2" x ¾" piece of wood to the lower right front of the body, matching up the 2-inch portion of the wood to the broken line on the lower right front of the body. The attached wood will extend about ¼" below the body.

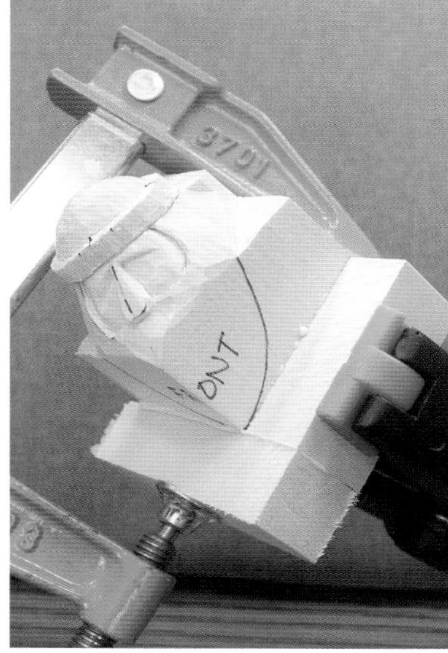
ONT

step 20

Now, glue the ⅞" x 3" x ¾" piece of wood to the lower left side of the body, matching the wood to the broken line on the lower left side of the body. The 3-inch piece will overlap the 2-inch piece of wood that was just glued on the right side. These two attached pieces will be the skirt on Father Christmas' robe. Clamp the skirt pieces to the body while the glue dries overnight.

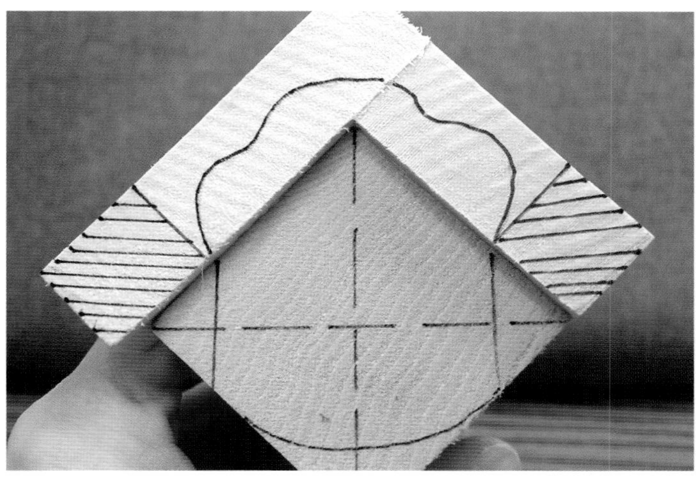

step 21

Next, the shaded areas to the far right and far left side of the newly added skirt pieces will be removed.

step 22

Score the wood to make a stop cut.

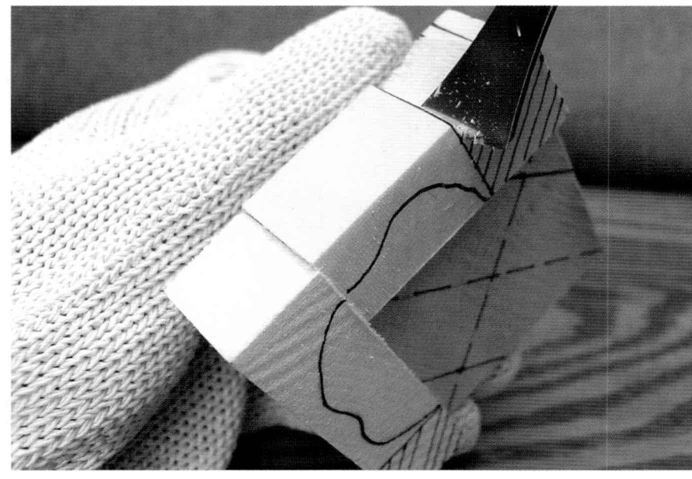

step 23

Then use a gouge to remove the wood up to the stop cut.

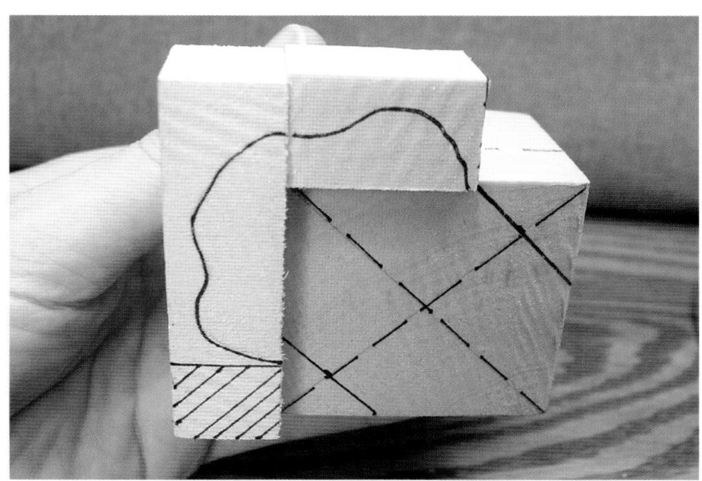

step 24

With one side removed, the block for the skirt will look like this.

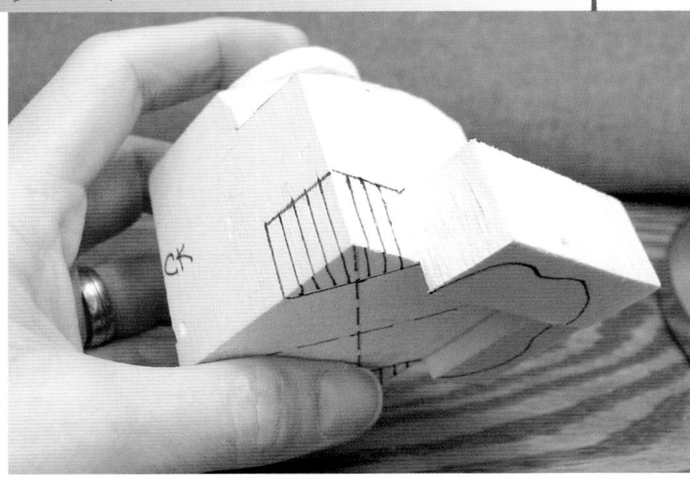

step 25 The wood in the shaded areas below the elbows will now be removed.

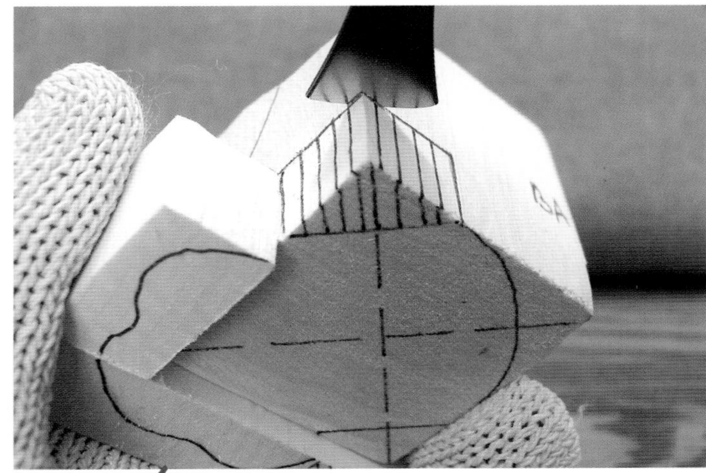

step 26 Create a stop cut at the elbow line by pushing the gouge into the corner of the piece.

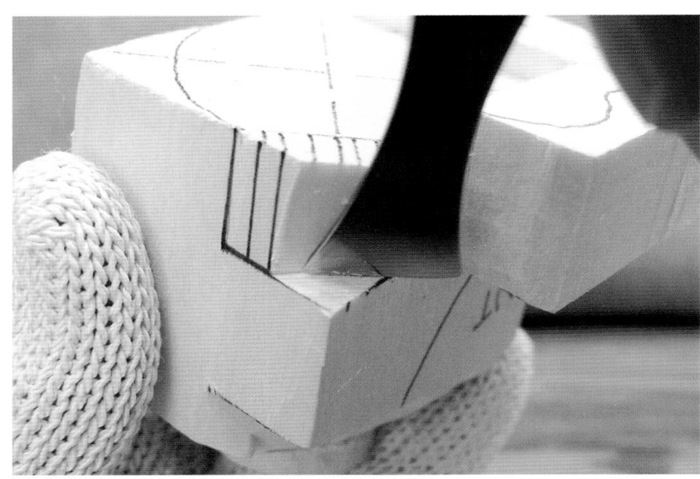

step 27 Remove the wood in a triangular fashion.

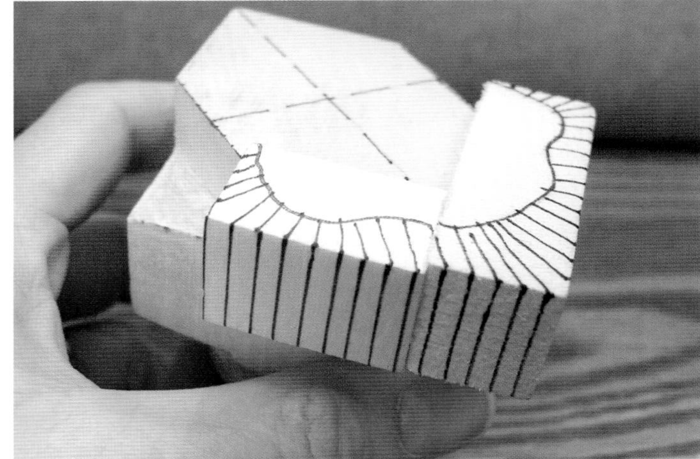

step 28 The progress to this point.

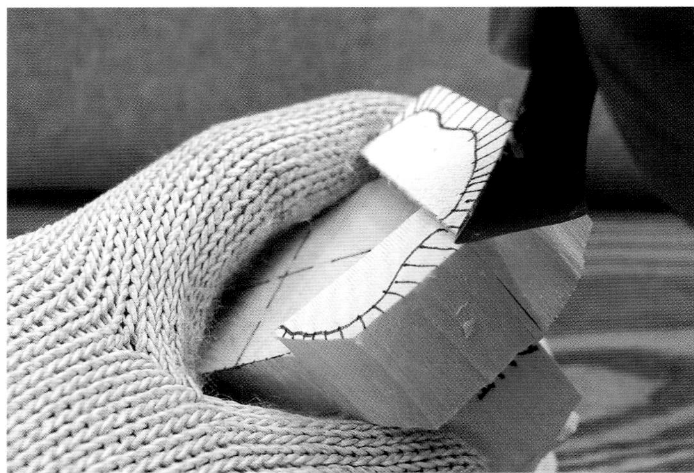

step 29 Remove the wood from this area with a gouge.

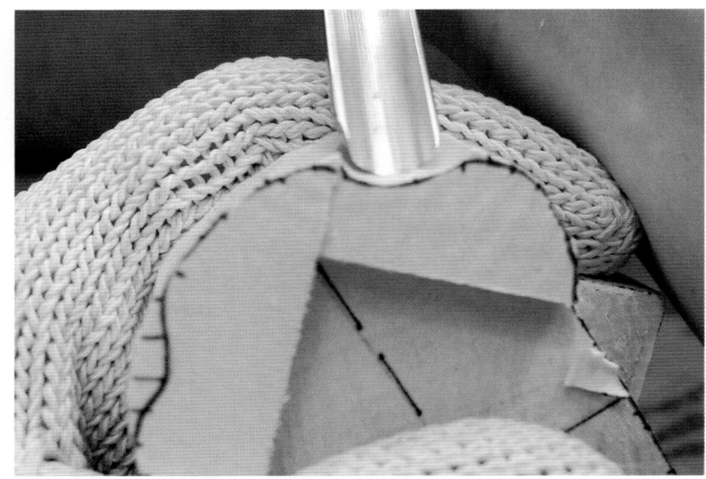

step 30 A 10mm, #9 gouge works well for creating a nice curve in the skirt.

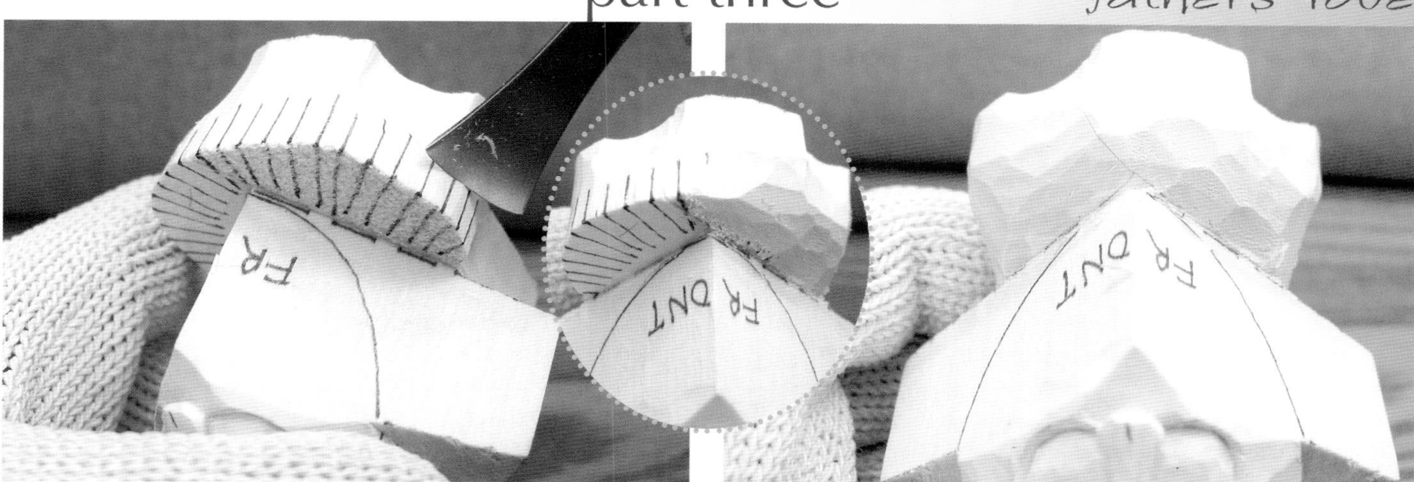

step 31 Turn the piece over and continue to round the top part of the skirt with the gouge.

step 32 Your progress to this point.

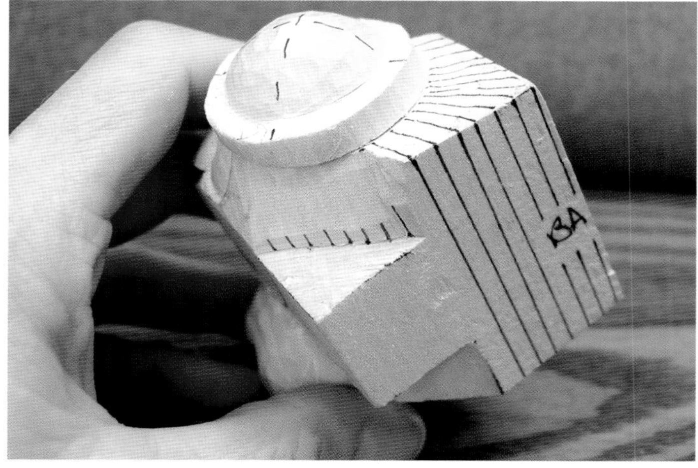

step 33 The shaded area will be removed next.

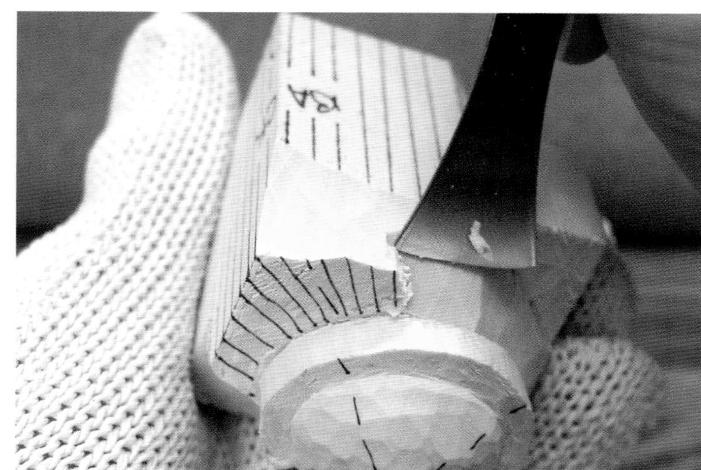

step 34 Carve up to the bottom of the wreath at an angle, pulling what will be his hair up under the wreath.

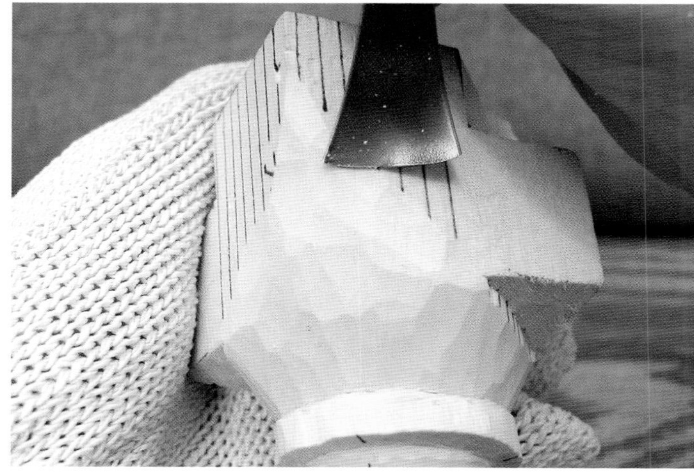

step 35 Continue removing wood from the entire back.

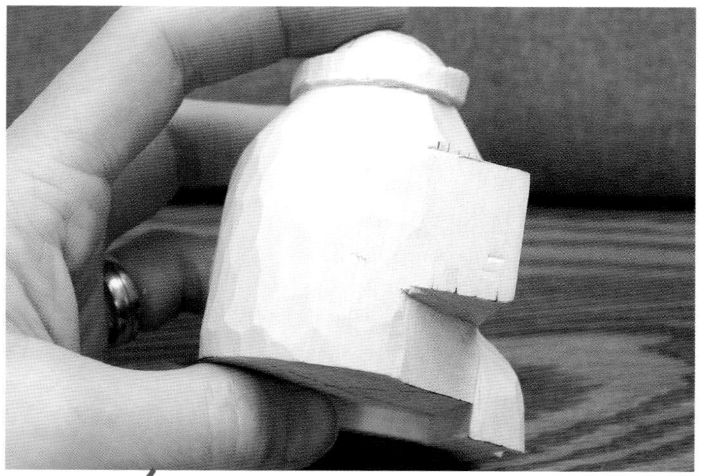

step 36 This photo shows the back nicely rounded.

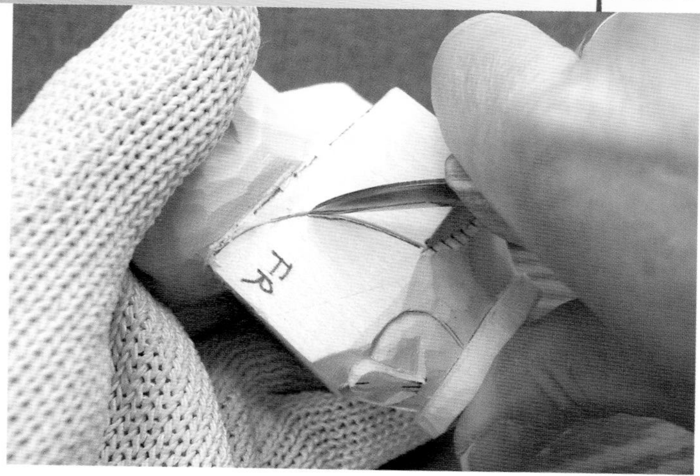
FR

step 37 Score around Father Christmas' beard with a cutting knife.

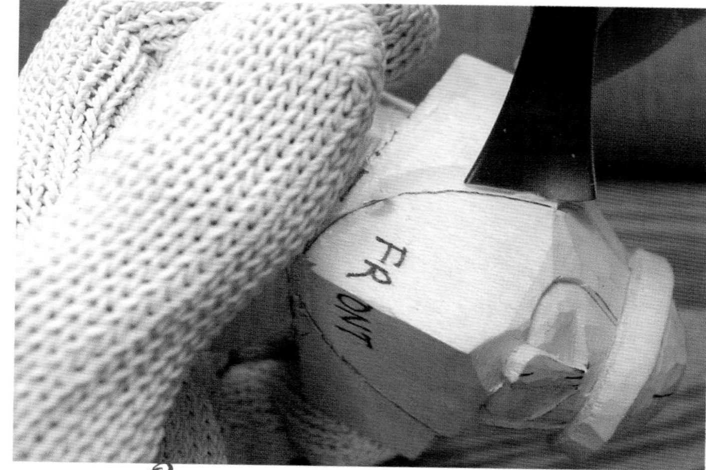
FR
ONT

step 38 Remove a small amount of wood underneath the beard.

step 39 Round the front edge of the beard.

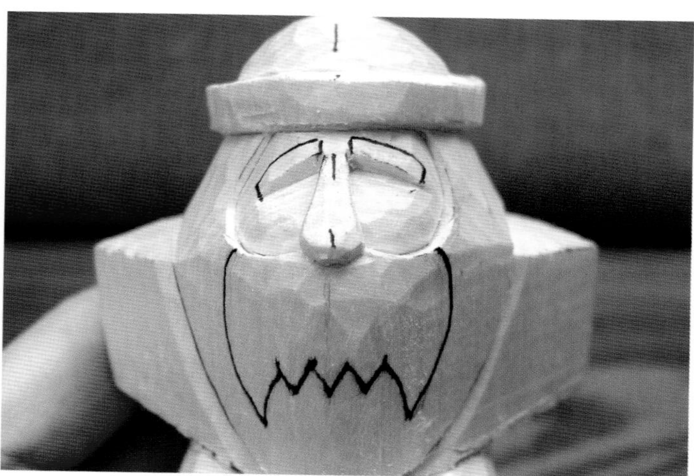

step 40 Draw in the moustache and eyebrows.

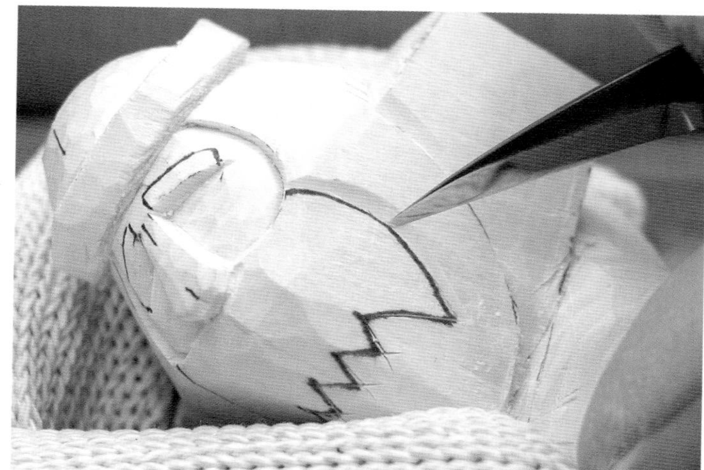

step 41 Score these lines; then remove a small amount of wood outside the moustache and eyebrows to define them.

step 42 The cuts to this point will look like this.

Father's hairline

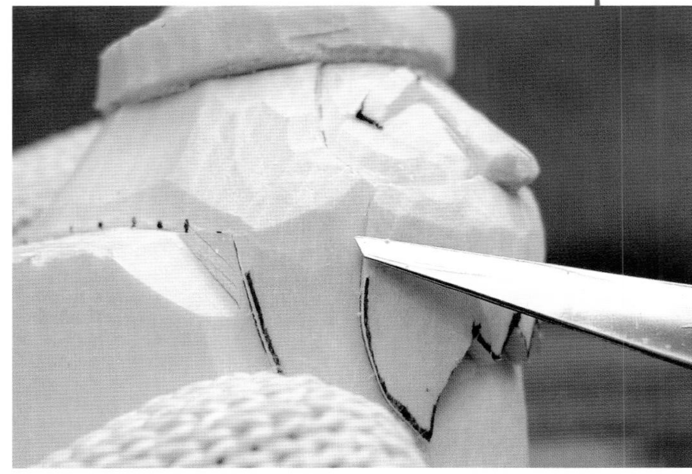

step 43 Round the edges on the sides of the moustache and refine the bottom edge of the moustache.

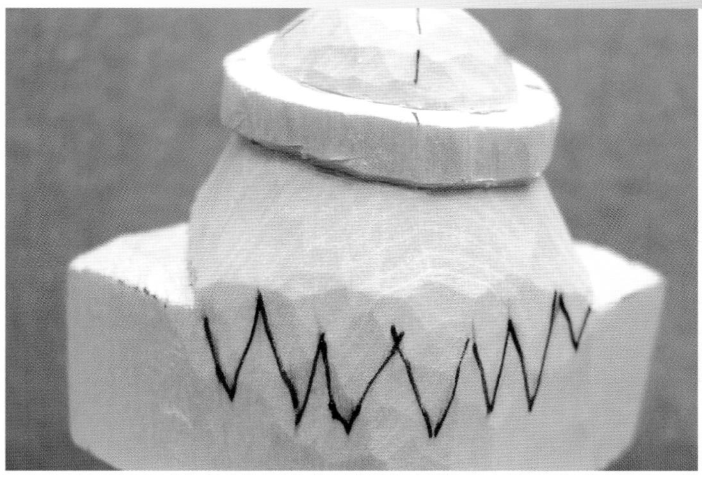

step 44 Draw in the back hairline on Father Christmas.

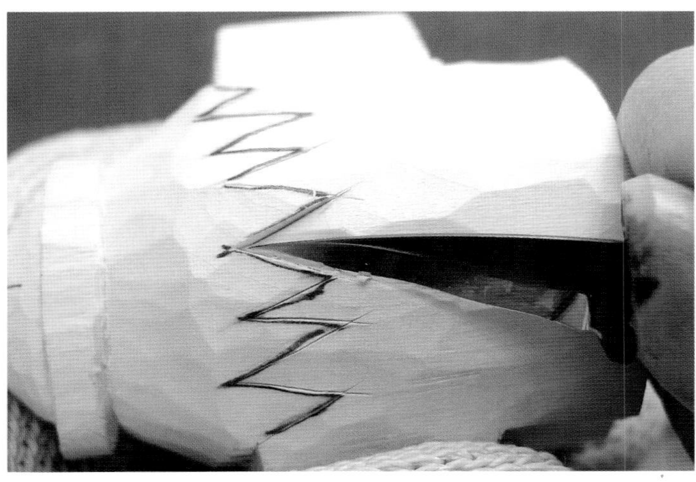

step 45 Score these lines and remove a small amount of wood underneath the hairline to define it.

Father's arms

step 46 Transfer the arm patterns to the two 1½" x ¾" x ¾" wood pieces. With a coping saw or gouge, remove the shaded triangular piece of wood on each arm.

step 47 Score the cuff line on all sides of the wood. Remove wood in the shaded area.

step 48 Score around the three sides of the thumb.

step 49 Remove enough wood to give the thumb a depth of ⅛".

step 50 Redraw the remaining hand pattern; then remove the wood outside the hand pattern in very flat planes.

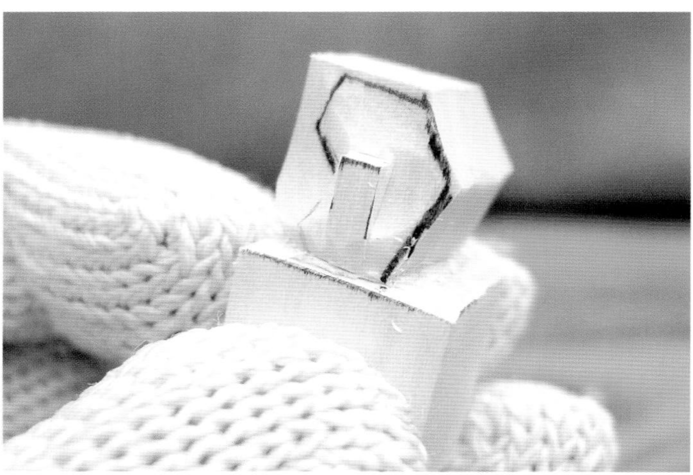

step 51 The resulting cuts leave the block looking like this.

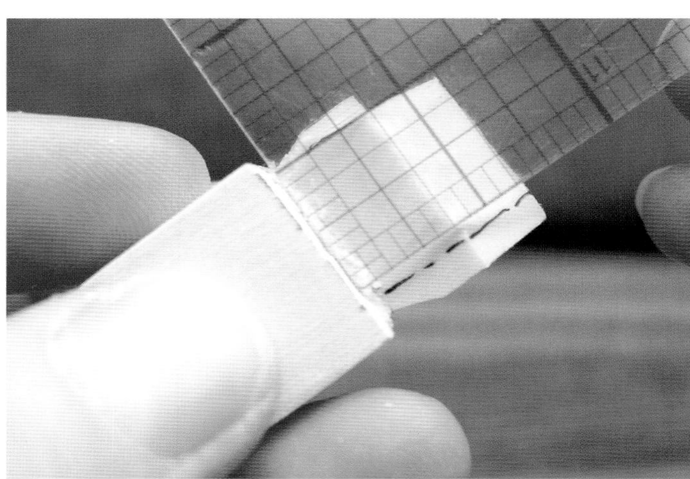

step 52 Trim the side of the hand opposite the thumb to a width of ½".

step 53 Draw in the line on the palm side of the hand. Score the line and remove the wood in the shaded area.

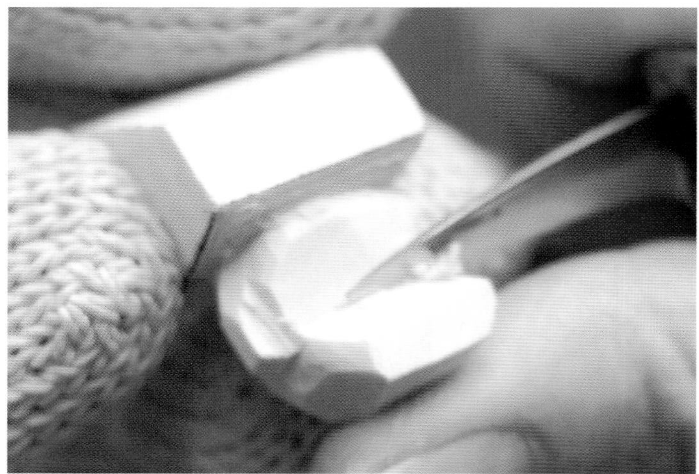

step 54 Carve out a recess in the palm area.

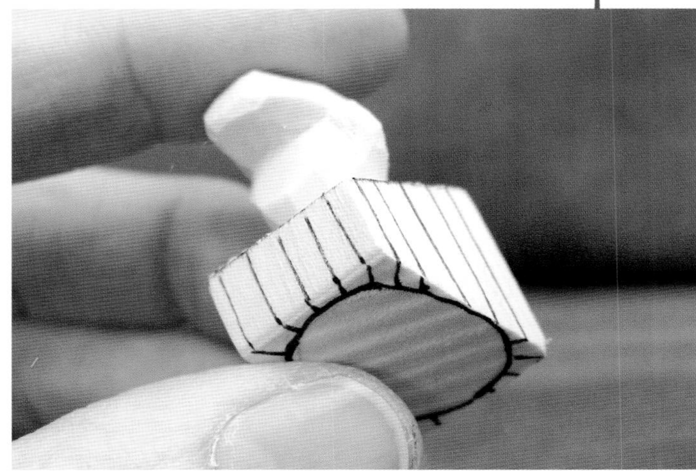

step 55 The shaded area shows the wood to be removed in the next step.

step 56 Carve away the wood outside the sleeve's circle.

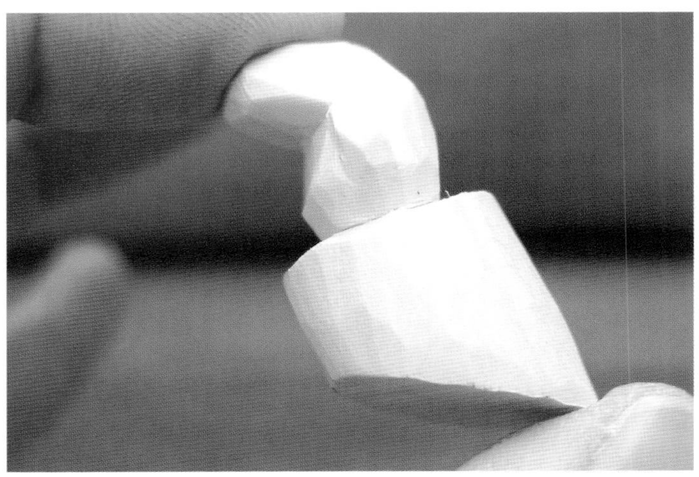

step 57 The final result will look like this. Repeat these steps on the other arm piece.

step 58 Using Carpenter's glue, attach the arm pieces to the lower part of the arms on the body. Allow the glue to dry overnight.

step 59 With a gouge, round and blend the shaded shoulder area. Also blend the area where the arms were glued to the body.

step 60 Draw in the front under-arm line.

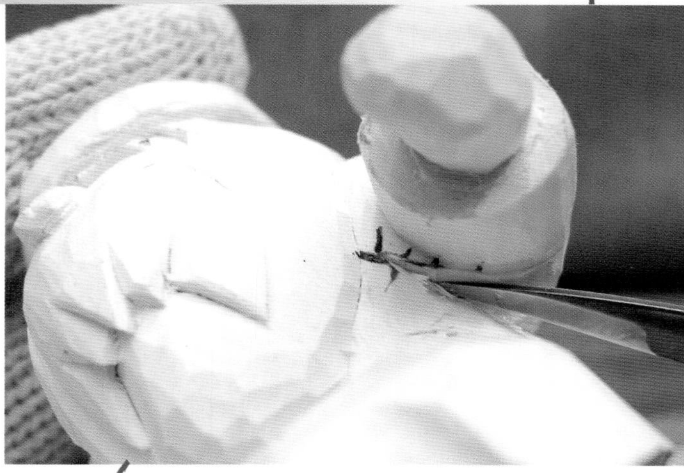

step 61 Score this line and remove wood from both sides to create a shallow trench. Repeat this process under the other arm.

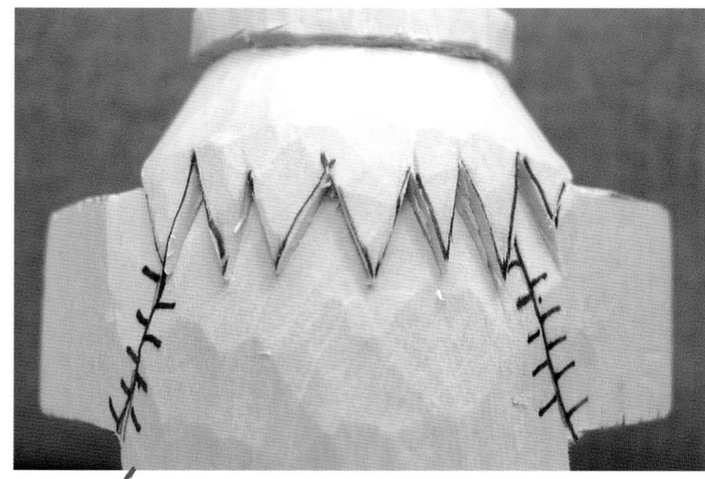

step 62 Draw the arm lines on the back of the piece.

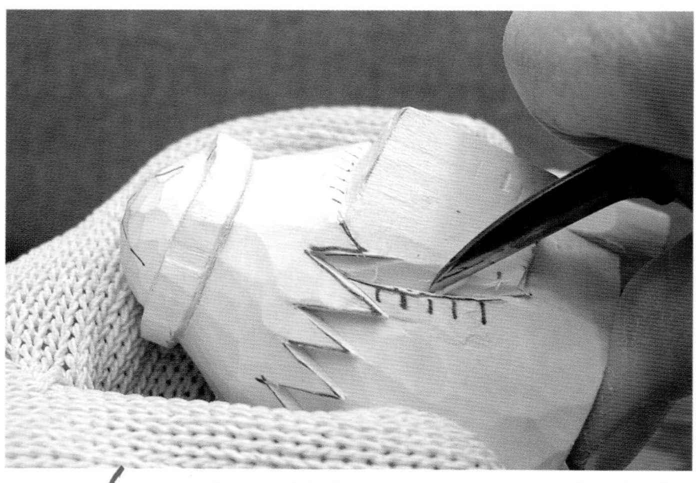

step 63 Score this line and remove wood on both sides of the line to create a shallow trench. Repeat this process on the other arm.

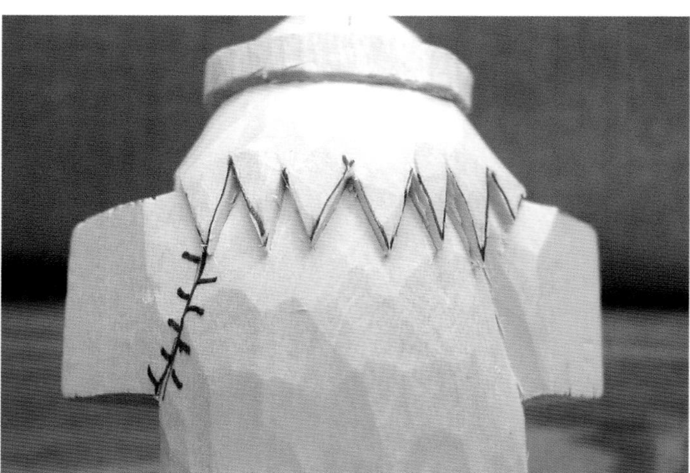

step 64 One line that separates the arm from the back is finished; the other has yet to be carved.

step 65 Draw the belt and the robe edge on the wood.

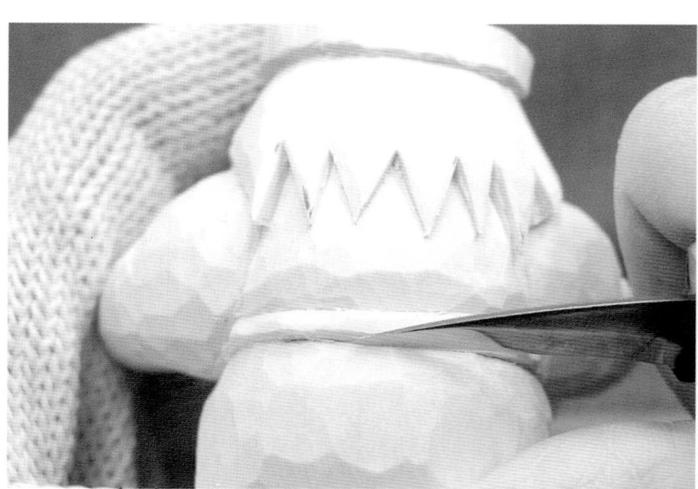

step 66 Score these lines and remove wood on both sides of the belt. Be sure to round the edges of the belt.

step 67 Draw diagonal lines on the belt. Score these lines and remove small slices of wood to give it a rope-like quality.

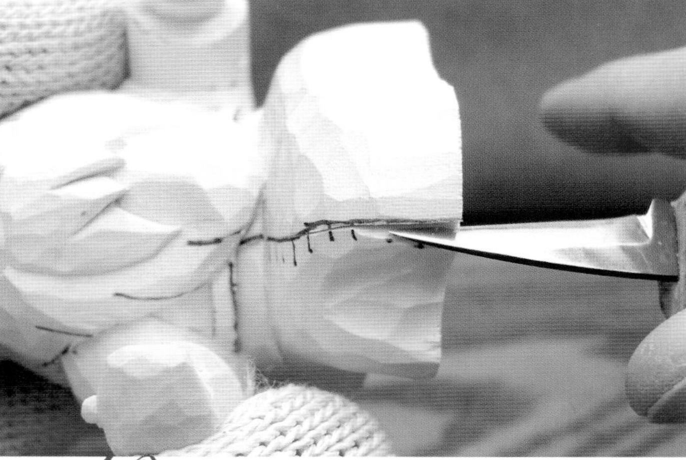

step 68 Remove the wood in the shaded area to the left of the robe edge.

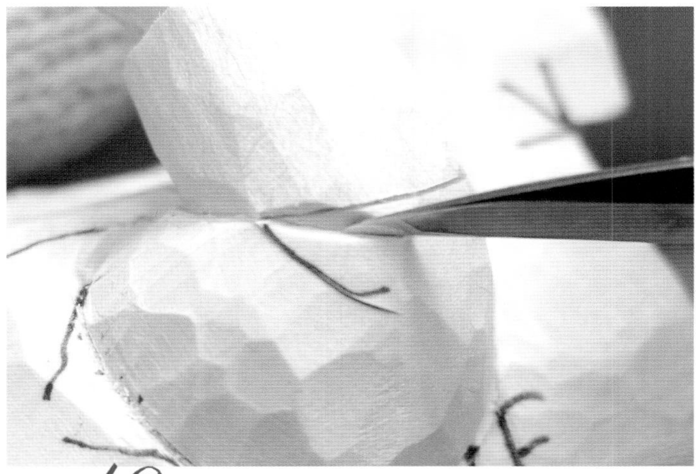

step 69 Draw in the outer elbow creases and the strand lines on the beard. Score these lines and remove small slices of wood on both sides of the score lines to further define these areas.

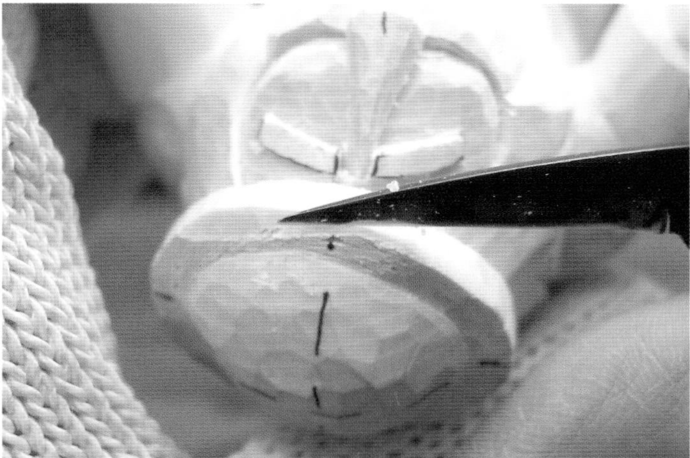

step 70 Round the edges of the wreath with a knife.

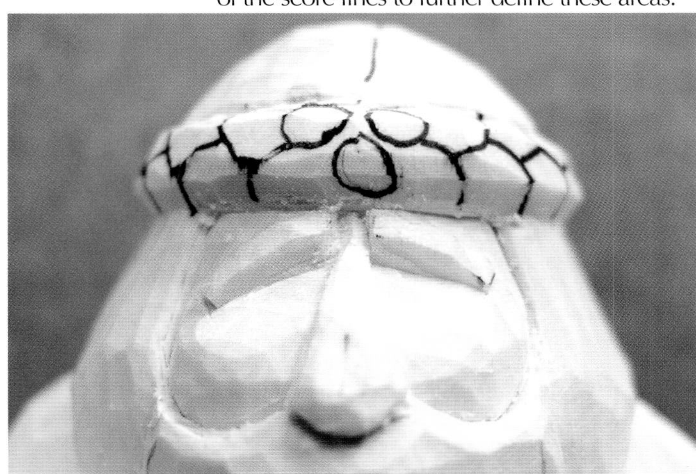

step 71 Draw the berries and the leaf design on the wreath.

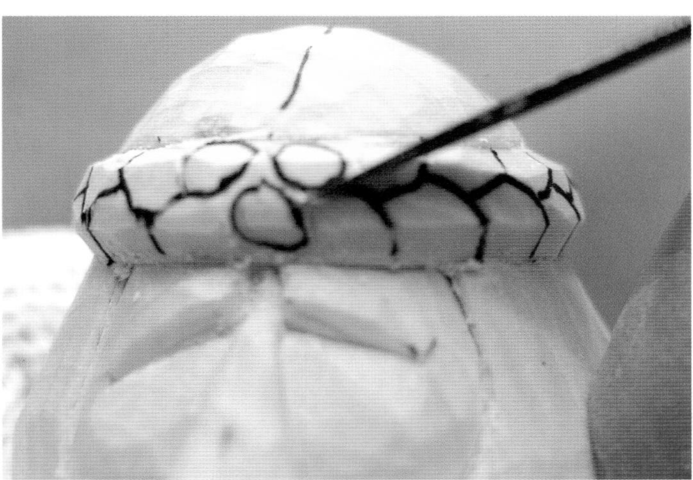

step 72 Score these lines and remove a small amount of wood around the berries.

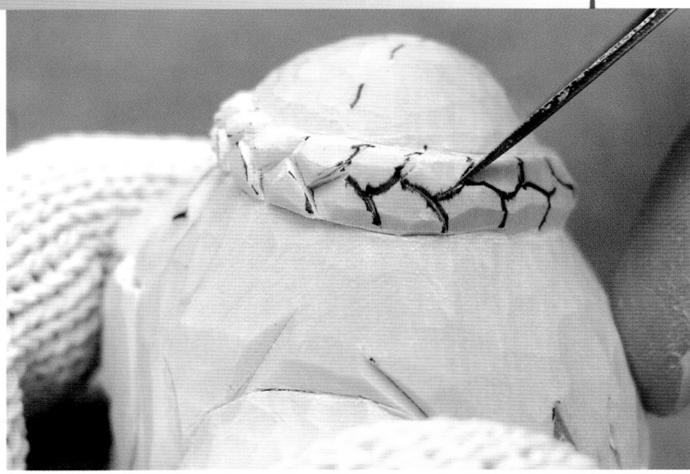

step 73 Score around the leaves and remove wood on the outside of each leaf with a detail knife to give definition to the wreath.

step 74 Draw the hairline above the wreath. Score the line and remove a small amount of wood above the scored line to give definition to the hairline.

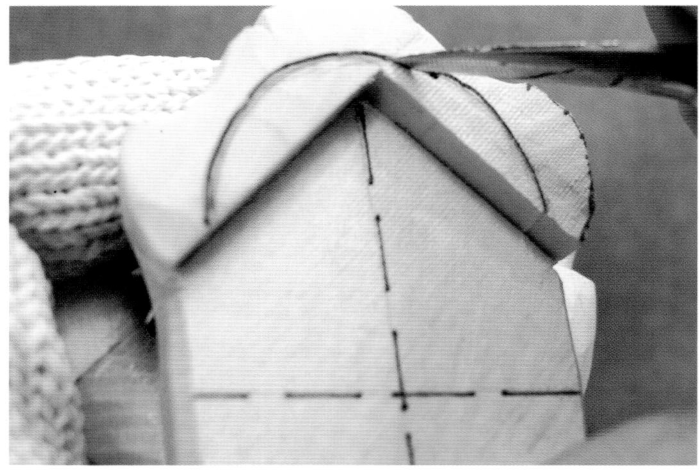

step 75 Draw in the semi-circle on the underskirt; then score this line with a cutting knife.

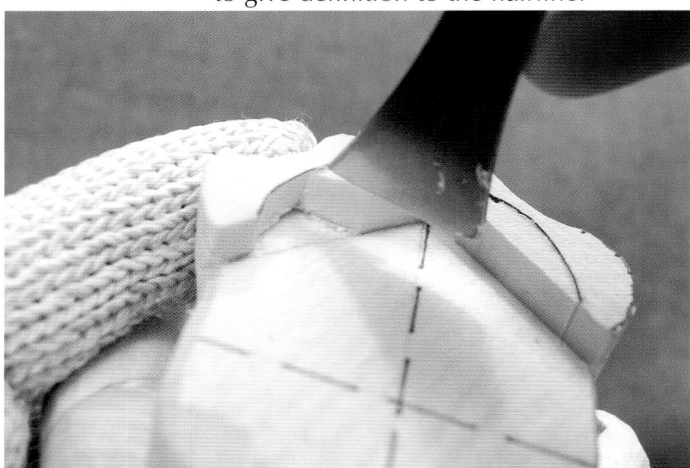

step 76 Remove the wood inside the inner circle with a gouge.

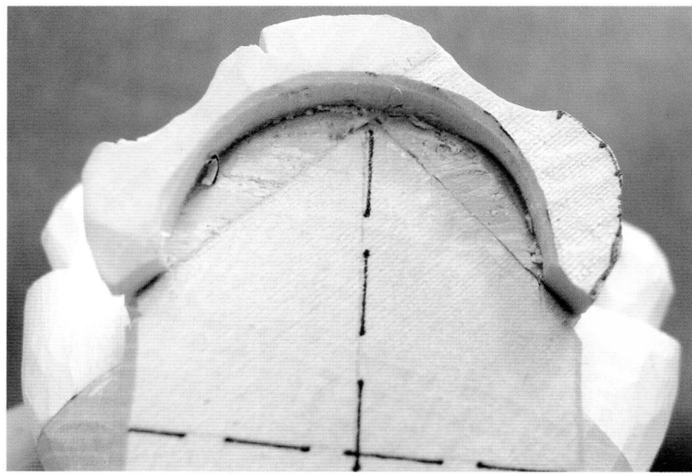

step 77 The result will look like this.

step 78 Transfer the pattern onto the two ¾ in. by 1 in. by ⅝ in. pieces of wood. Remember to flip the boot pattern so you have both a right and a left boot.

step 79 Remove the wood in the shaded area.

step 80 Round the wood in the shaded area outside the bottom boot pattern.

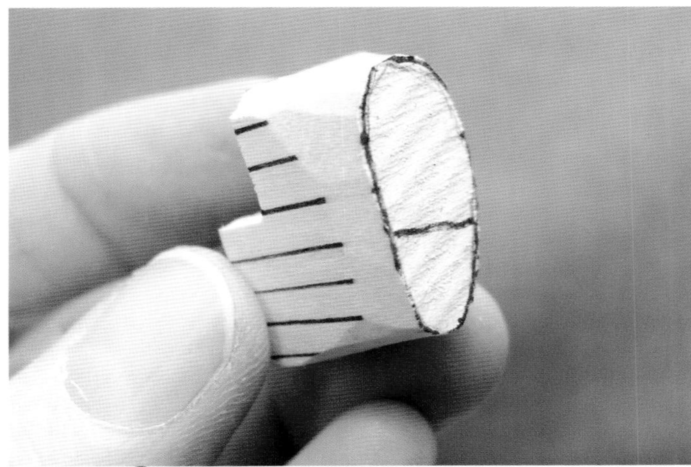

step 81 The boot to this point.

step 82 Round the leg and toe of the boot using stop cuts as needed.

step 83 The result will look like this.

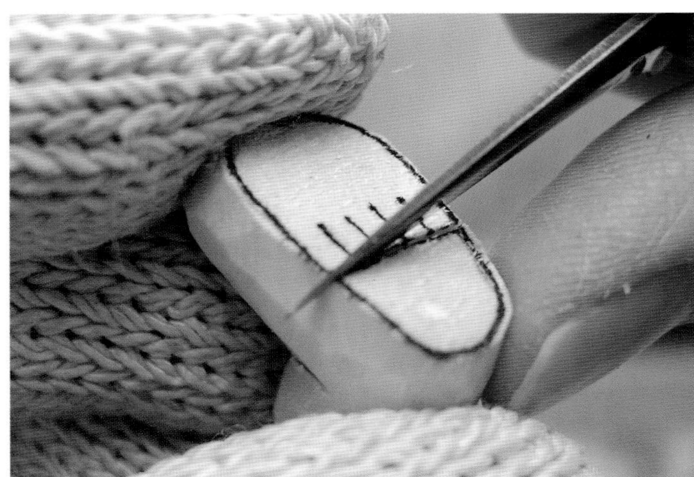

step 84 Score the line for the heel of the boot.

step 85 Remove the wood at a diagonal in the shaded area to define the heel of the boot.

step 86 Draw the sole of the boot. Score the line and remove a small amount of wood in the shaded area.

step 87 The finished boot.

step 88 Transfer the pattern to the top and bottom of the three ⅝" x ⅝" x ⅝" blocks.

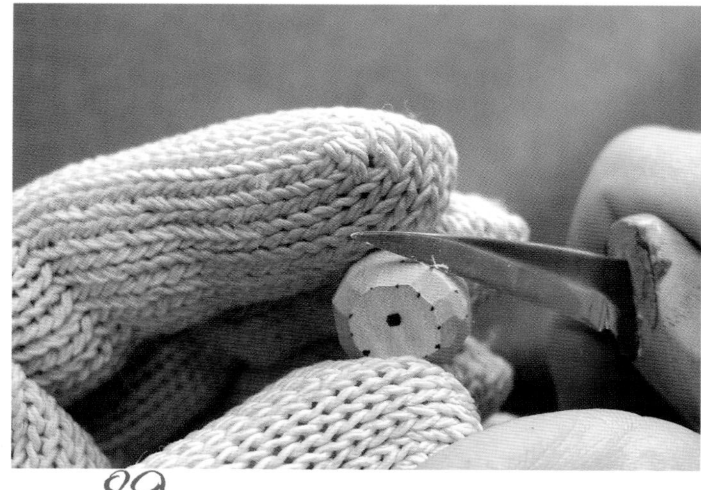

step 89 Remove the wood in the shaded area to round the apple.

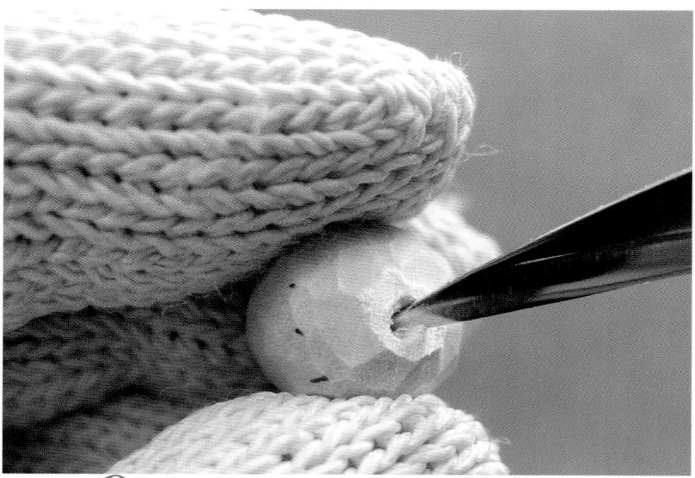

step 90 Insert the tip of the detail knife in the dot on the top of the apple.

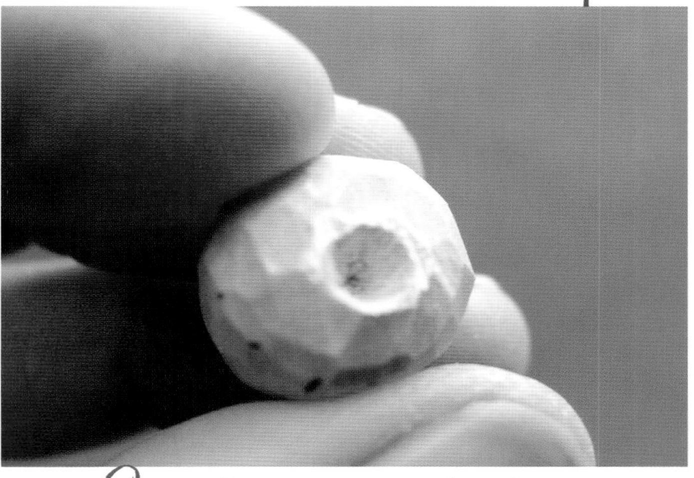

step 91 Carve out a narrow funnel approximately ⅛" deep. Cut another funnel, approximately 1⁄16" deep, on the bottom of the apple.

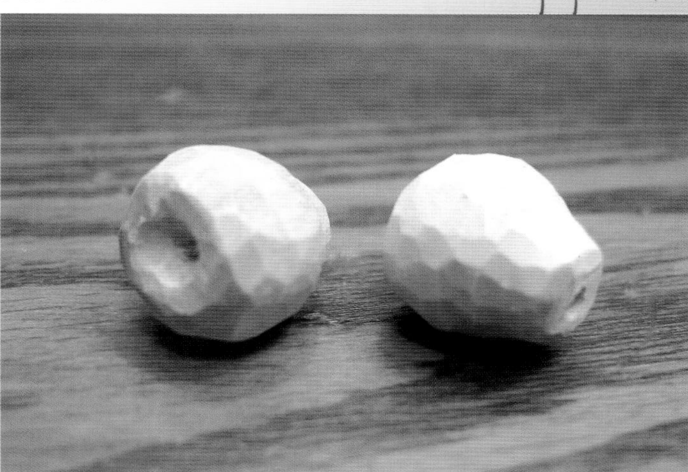

step 92 The finished apples.

step 93 Draw the apple stem pattern on the large end of a wooden sandwich pick.

step 94 With a detail knife, carve the curve in the stem. Remove the rest of the wood outside the pattern.

step 95 Rolling a 1⁄16" drill bit between your fingers, gently drill a hole in the apple stem. Cut off the remaining pick now or after the stem is painted. Now Father Christmas is ready to assemble and paint.

•part three•

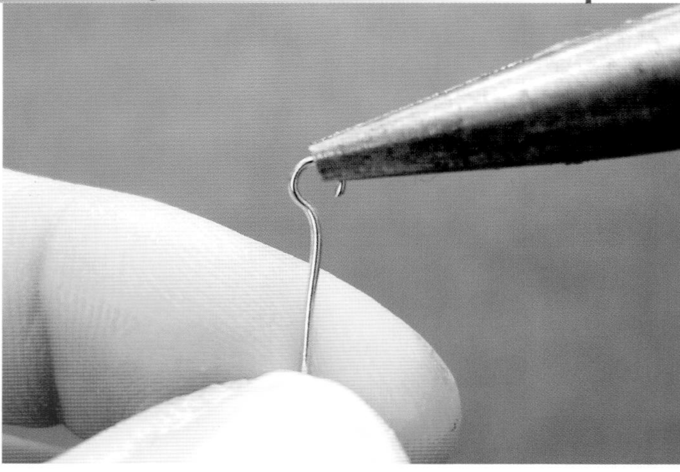

step 1 Using needle nose pliers, pull open the eye end of an eye pin.

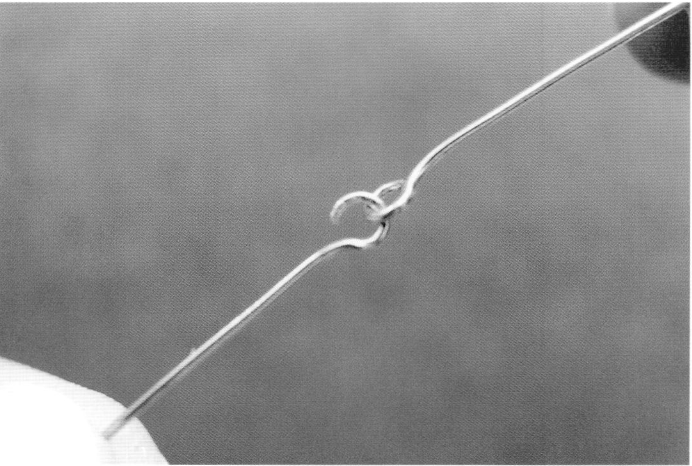

step 2 Thread a second eye pin onto the open eye pin.

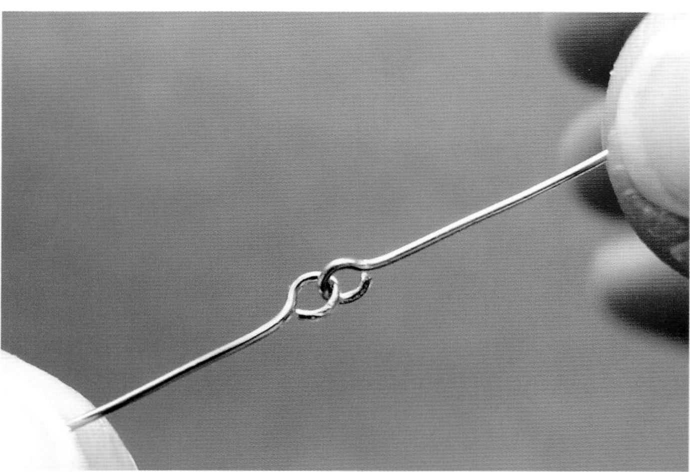

step 3 With pliers, close the first eye pin. This forms the eye pin joint. Trim the straight wire beneath the eye part of the pin to ¼".

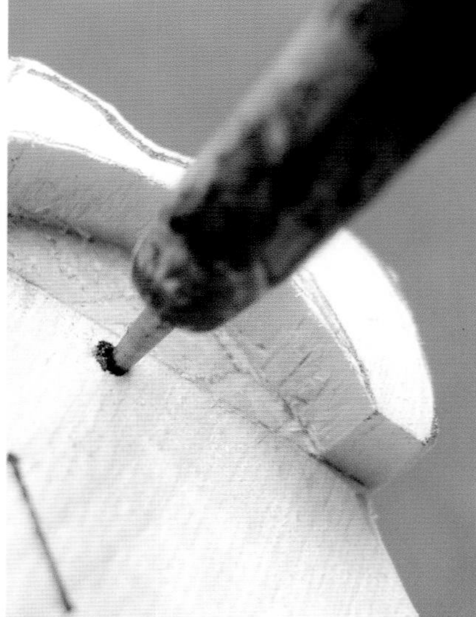

step 4 After Santa is painted insert a stylus to a depth of ¼in. at the dots on the underskirt to form pilot holes. (Shown here on unpainted wood for photographic purposes.)

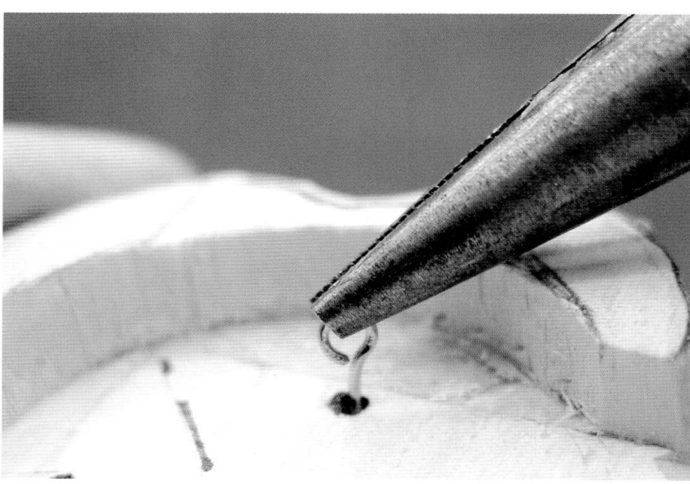

step 5 Add a drop of instant glue to the pilot hole and insert one straight end of the eye pin joint into the hole.

step 6 Allow the glue a few minutes to completely set up. Repeat the process on the second hole.

step 7 Paint the boots, then insert the stylus into the dot on the top of the boots to a depth of approximately ¼".

step 8 Turn Father Christmas right side up and align the remaining straight end of the eye pin joint with the pilot hole on the boot. Add a drop of instant glue to the hole in the top of the boot. Insert the straight end of the eye pin in the pilot hole and hold for 30 seconds to allow time for the glue to bond the two pieces. Repeat for the other boot.

step 9 Paint the apples and Santa according to the directions on page 70. Glue the stem to the top of the apple with instant glue.

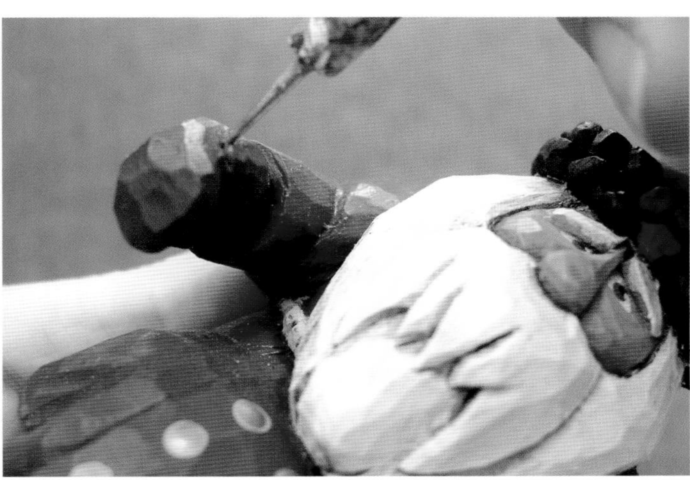

step 10 Using a stylus, push pilot holes into Father Christmas' hands on the outsides of his thumbs.

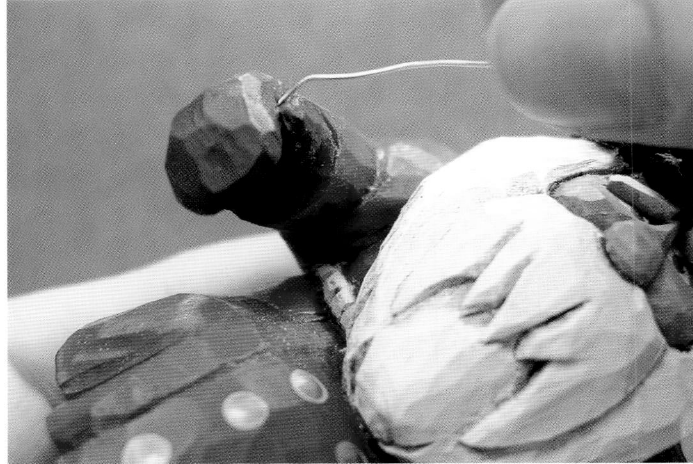

step 11 Place a dot of instant glue on the pilot hole on his left mitten; then insert a 3-in. length of 24-gauge brass wire into the left pilot hole.

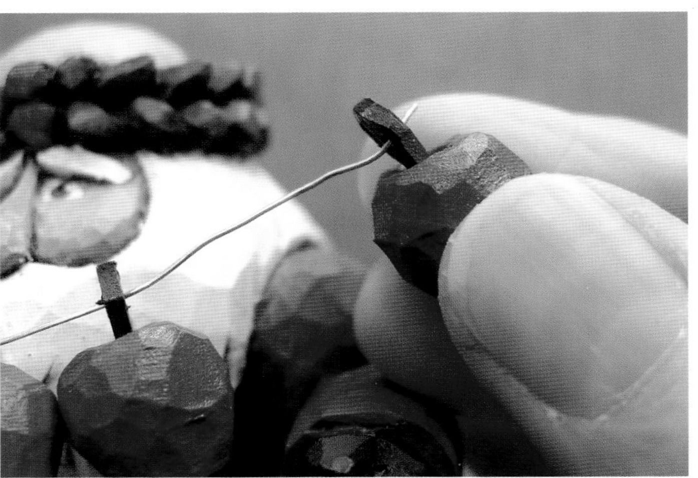

step 12 Thread the apples onto the wire. Shorten the wire length if necessary and glue the remaining end of the wire behind the thumb on the right mitten.

FATHER CHRISTMAS
ENGLAND

THE COLOR CHART

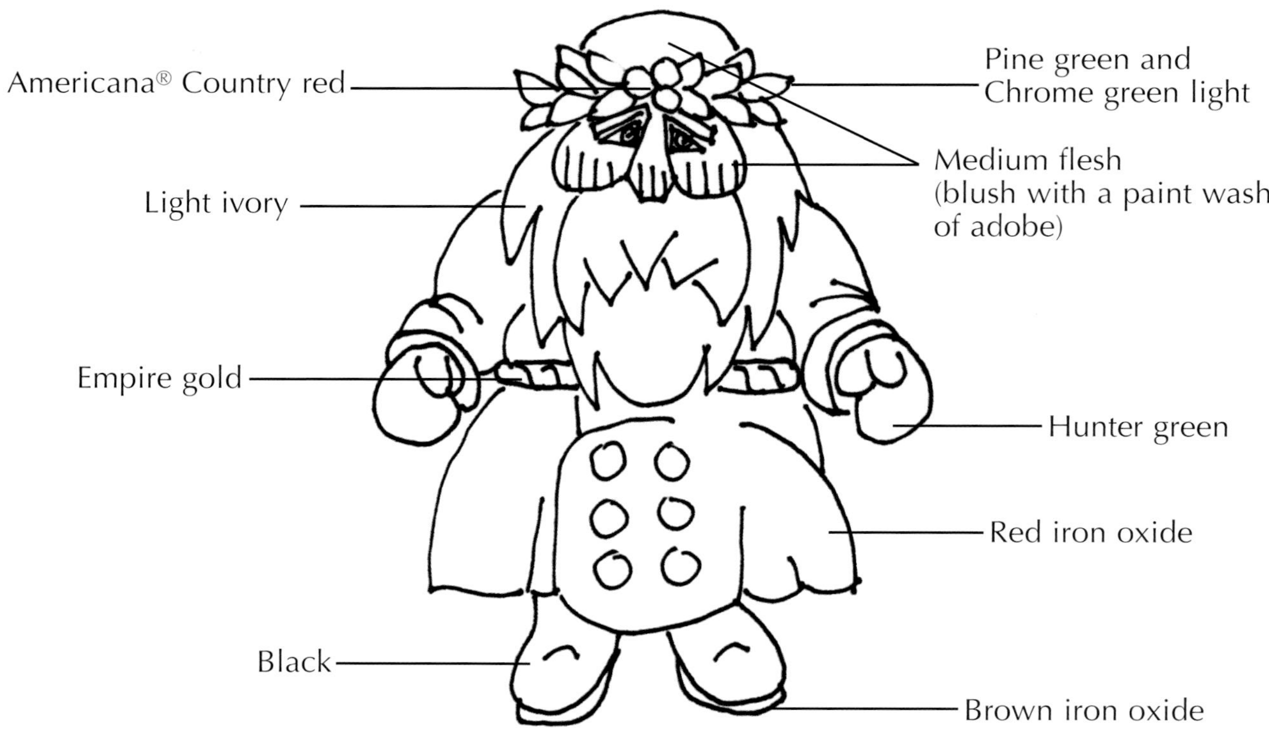
Americana® Country red
Light ivory
Empire gold
Black
Pine green and
Chrome green light
Medium flesh
(blush with a paint wash
of adobe)
Hunter green
Red iron oxide
Brown iron oxide

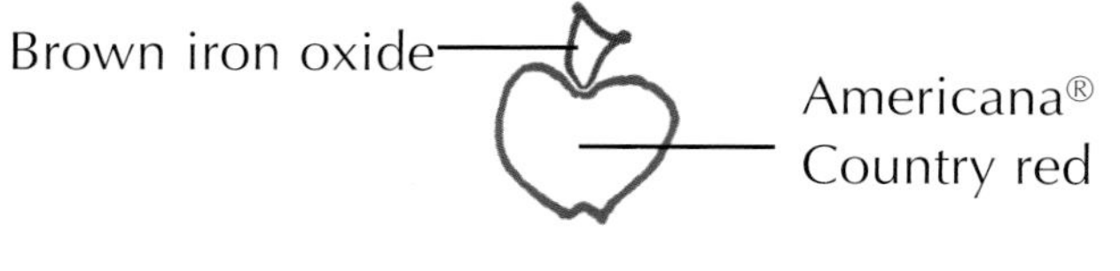
Brown iron oxide
Americana®
Country red

Button detail

1) Empire gold dot

2) metallic gold dot

All colors manufactured by Delta Ceramcoat® unless otherwise noted.

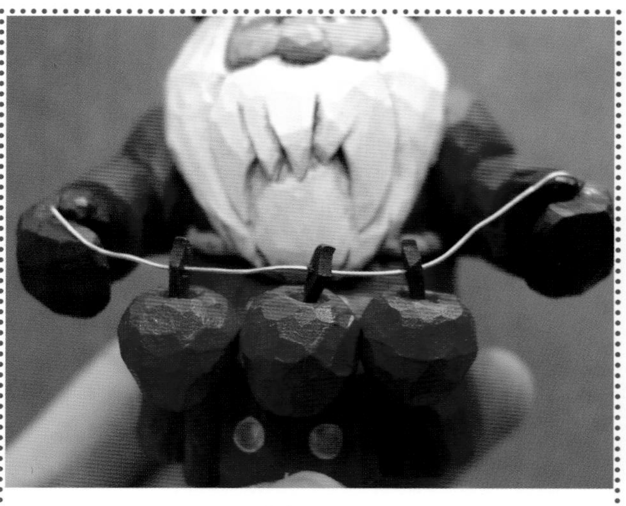

NOW FATHER CHRISTMAS IS READY TO SIT ON YOUR FAVORITE SHELF OR MANTLE.

Belsnickle Germany

Wood List

Body	1 ea.	3½" x 2" x 2"
Arms	2 ea.	1⅛" x ¾" x ¾"
Boots	2 ea.	¾" x 1" x ⅝"
Skirt	1 ea.	⅞" x 2" x ¾"
	1 ea.	⅞" x 3" x ¾"
Switch	1 ea.	twig
Eye Pins	4 ea.	

Paint List

Adobe
Brown iron oxide
Alpine green
Hunter green
Ivory
Light Ivory
Medium flesh
Raw sienna
Tuscan red

Belsnickle Germany

The Pattern

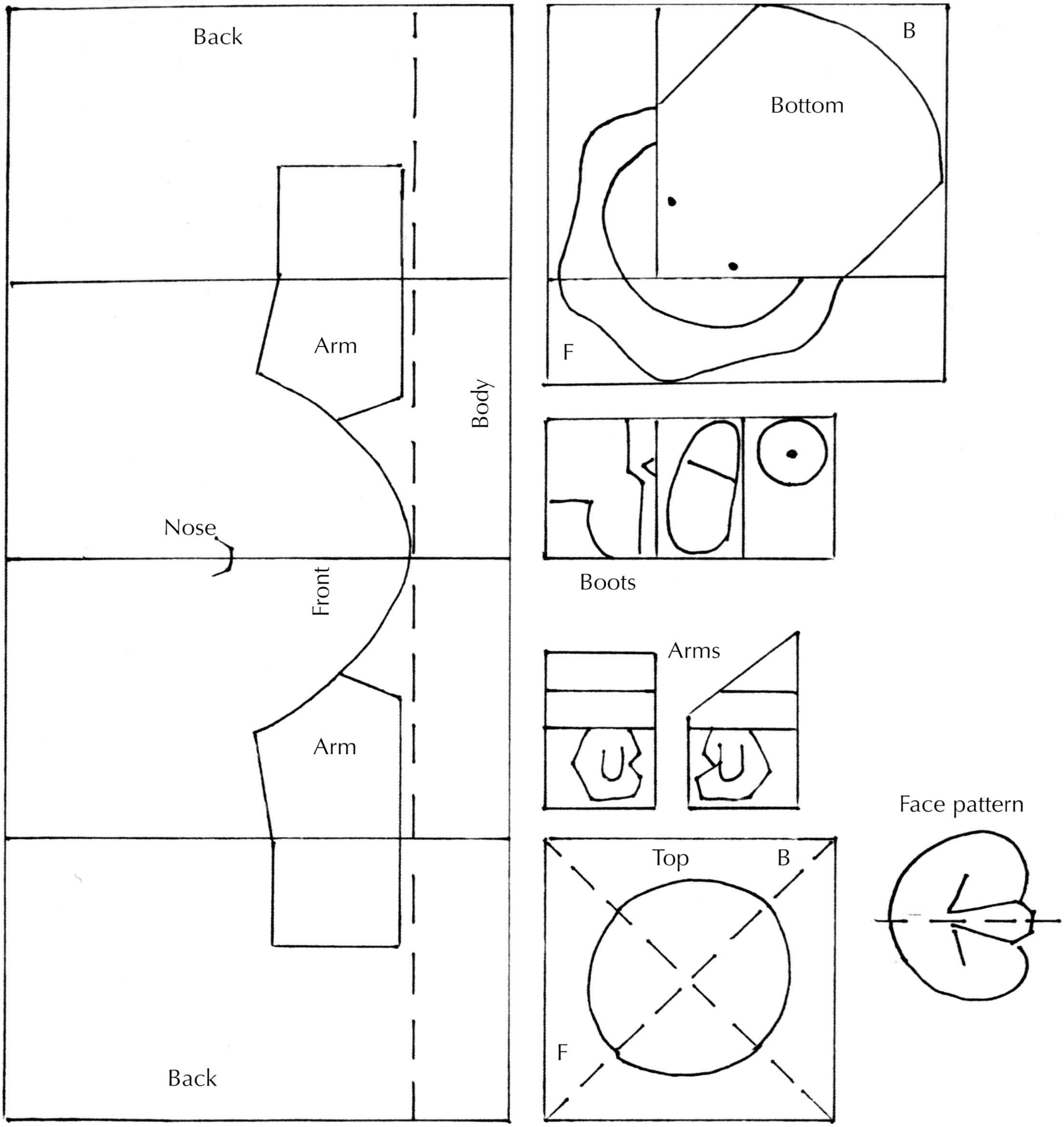

Back
Arm
Body
Nose
Front
Arm
Back
B
Bottom
F
Boots
Arms
Face pattern
Top
B
F

Belsnickle
Germany

The Color Chart

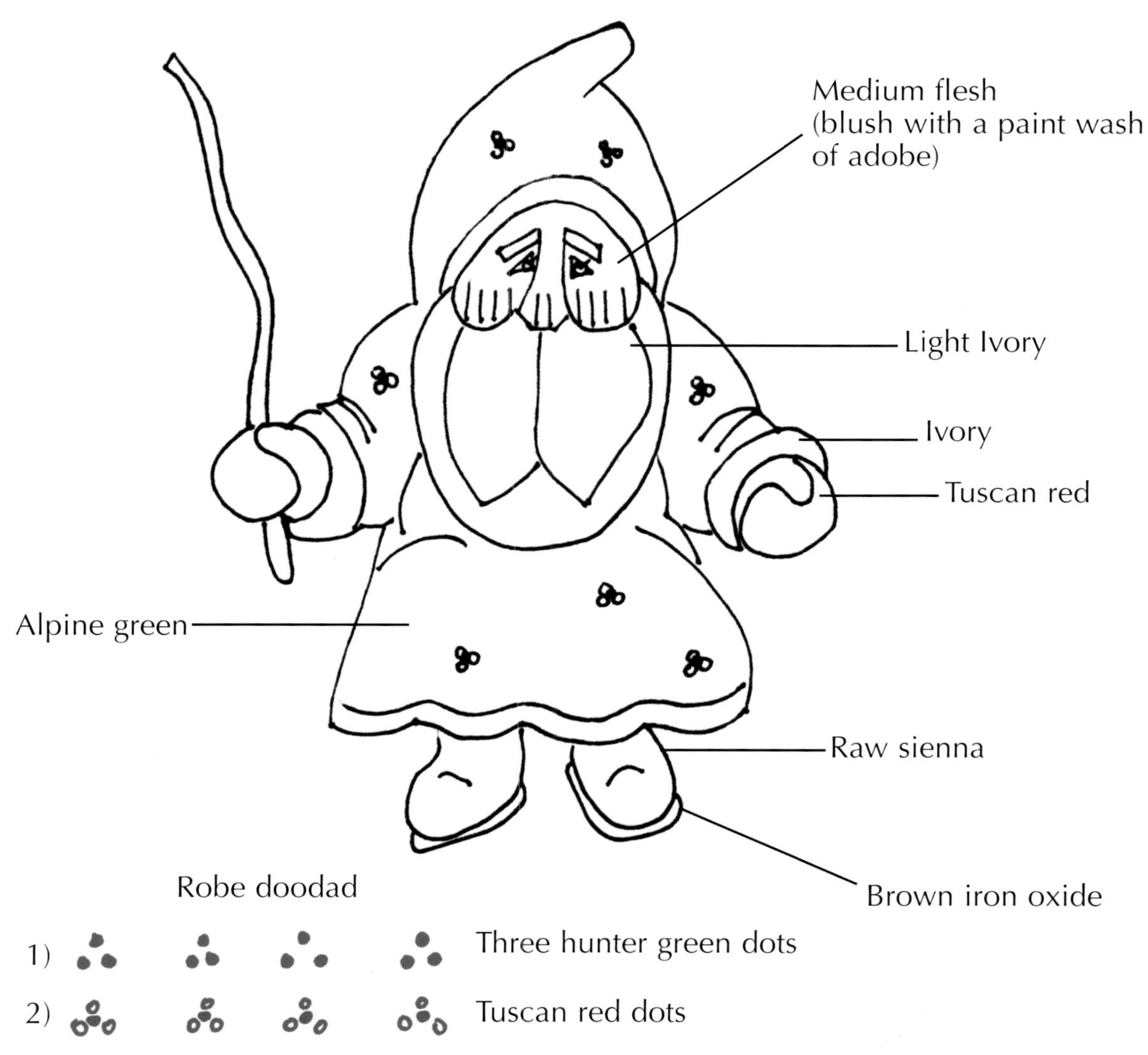
Medium flesh
(blush with a paint wash
of adobe)
Light Ivory
Ivory
Tuscan red
Alpine green
Raw sienna
Brown iron oxide

Robe doodad

1) Three hunter green dots

2) Tuscan red dots

Actual size

All colors manufactured by Delta Ceramcoat® unless otherwise noted.

•part three•

Bueller Clos
Northern Germany

Wood List

Body	1 ea.	3½" x 2" x 2"
Legs	1 ea.	⅞" x 2" x ¾"
	1 ea.	⅞" x 3" x ¾"
Arms	1 ea.	1½" x ¾" x ¾"
	1 ea.	1⅛" x ¾" x ¾"
Boots	2 ea.	¾" x 1" x ⅝"
Bag	1 ea.	1¼" x 1¼" x 1¼"
Bag Top	1 ea.	1" x ½" x ½"
Bell	1 ea.	1" x ⅜" x ⅜"
Bell Handle	1 ea.	1" x ⅜" x ⅜"
Eye Pins	4 ea.	

Paint List

Adobe
Black
Brown iron oxide
Chrome green light
Americana® Country red
Empire gold
Golden brown
Lichen grey
Light ivory
Medium flesh
Metallic silver
Nightfall blue
Pine green
Toffee
Tompte red

Bueller Clos Northern Germany

The Pattern

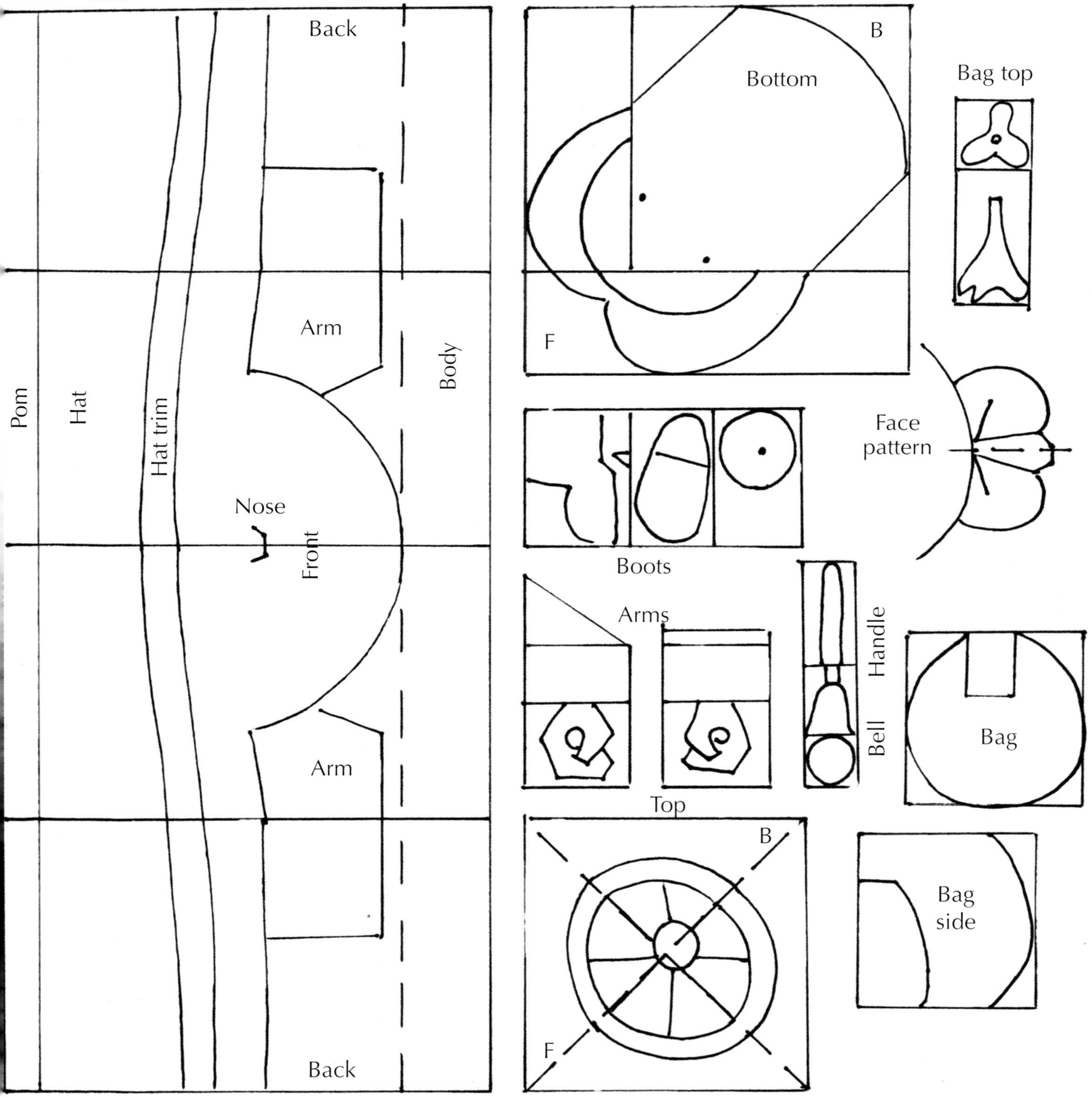

Back
Pom
Hat
Hat trim
Arm
Body
Nose
Front
Arm
Back
B
Bottom
F
Bag top
Face pattern
Boots
Arms
Handle
Bell
Bag
Top
B
F
Bag side

•part three•

Bueller Clos Northern Germany

The Color Chart

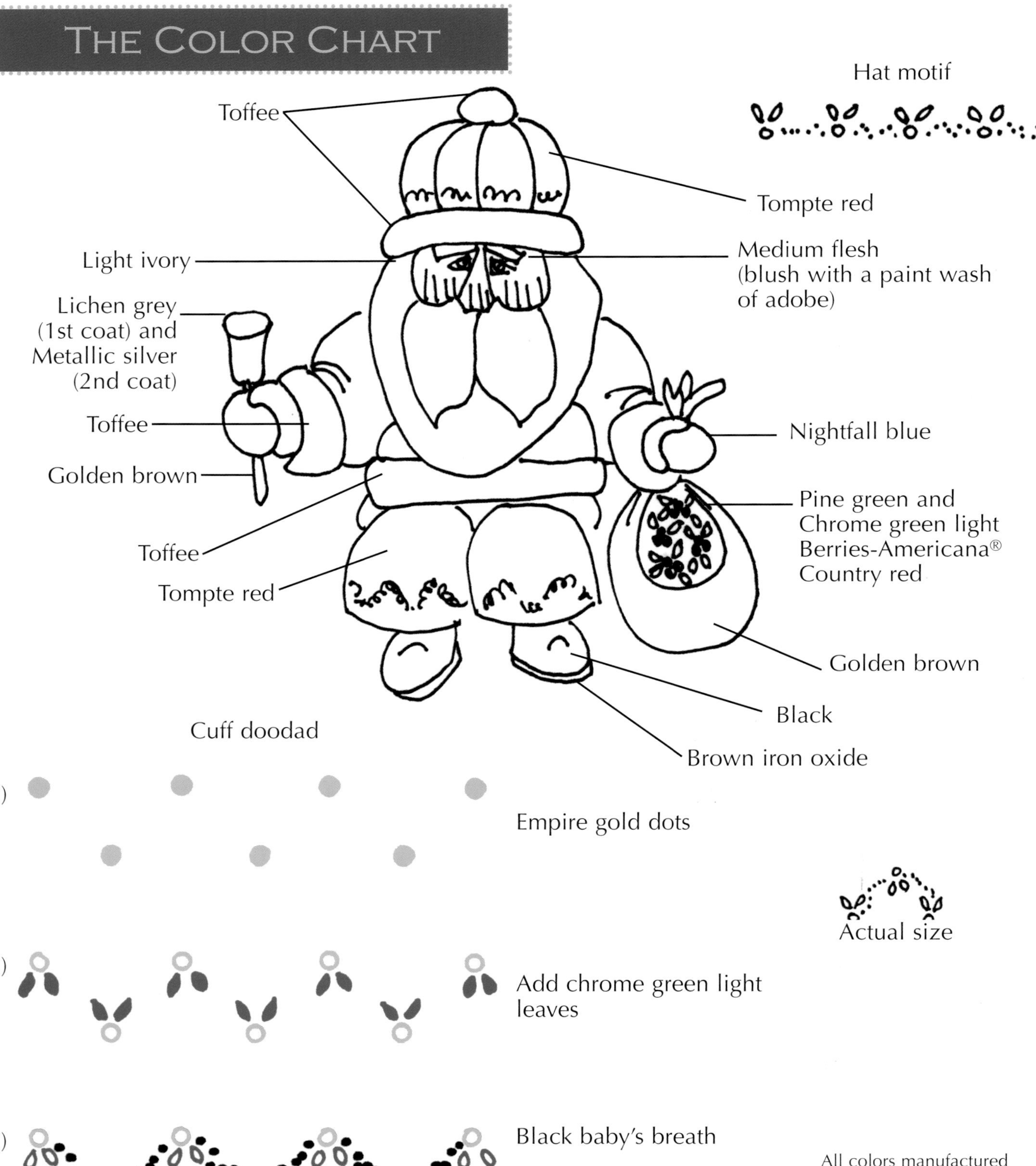
Hat motif
Toffee
Tompte red
Light ivory
Medium flesh (blush with a paint wash of adobe)
Lichen grey (1st coat) and Metallic silver (2nd coat)
Toffee
Nightfall blue
Golden brown
Pine green and Chrome green light Berries-Americana® Country red
Toffee
Tompte red
Golden brown
Black
Brown iron oxide
Cuff doodad
1)
Empire gold dots
Actual size
2)
Add chrome green light leaves
3)
Black baby's breath

All colors manufactured by Delta Ceramcoat® unless otherwise noted.

•part three•

Grandfather Frost
Russia

Wood List

Body	1 ea.	3" x 2" x 2"
Legs	1 ea.	⅞" x 2" x ¾"
	1 ea.	⅞" x 3" x ¾"
Arms	2 ea.	1" x 1½" x ¾"
Boots	2 ea.	¾" x 1" x ⅝"
Lower Staff	1 ea.	2" x ⅜" x ⅜"
Upper Staff	1 ea.	1" x ⅜" x ⅜"
Bag	1 ea.	1¼" x 1" x 1"
Bag Top	1 ea.	1"x ½" x ½"
Eye Pins	4 ea.	

Paint List

Adobe
Burnt umber
Golden brown
Light ivory
Maple sugar brown
Medium flesh
Old parchment
Raw sienna

GRANDFATHER FROST
RUSSIA

THE PATTERN

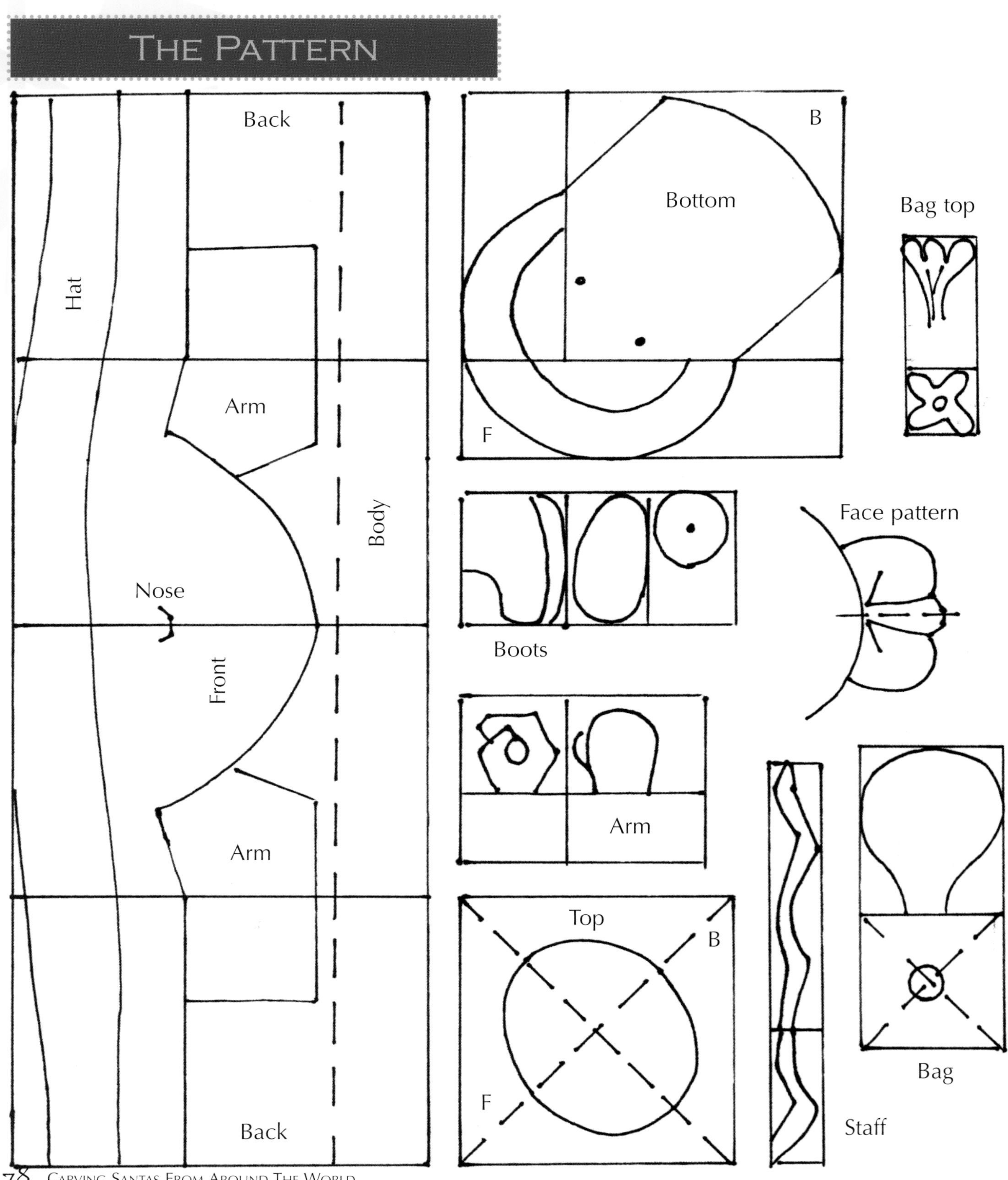
Back
Hat
Arm
Body
Nose
Front
Arm
Back
B
Bottom
F
Bag top
Boots
Face pattern
Arm
Top
B
F
Staff
Bag

GRANDFATHER FROST
RUSSIA

THE COLOR CHART

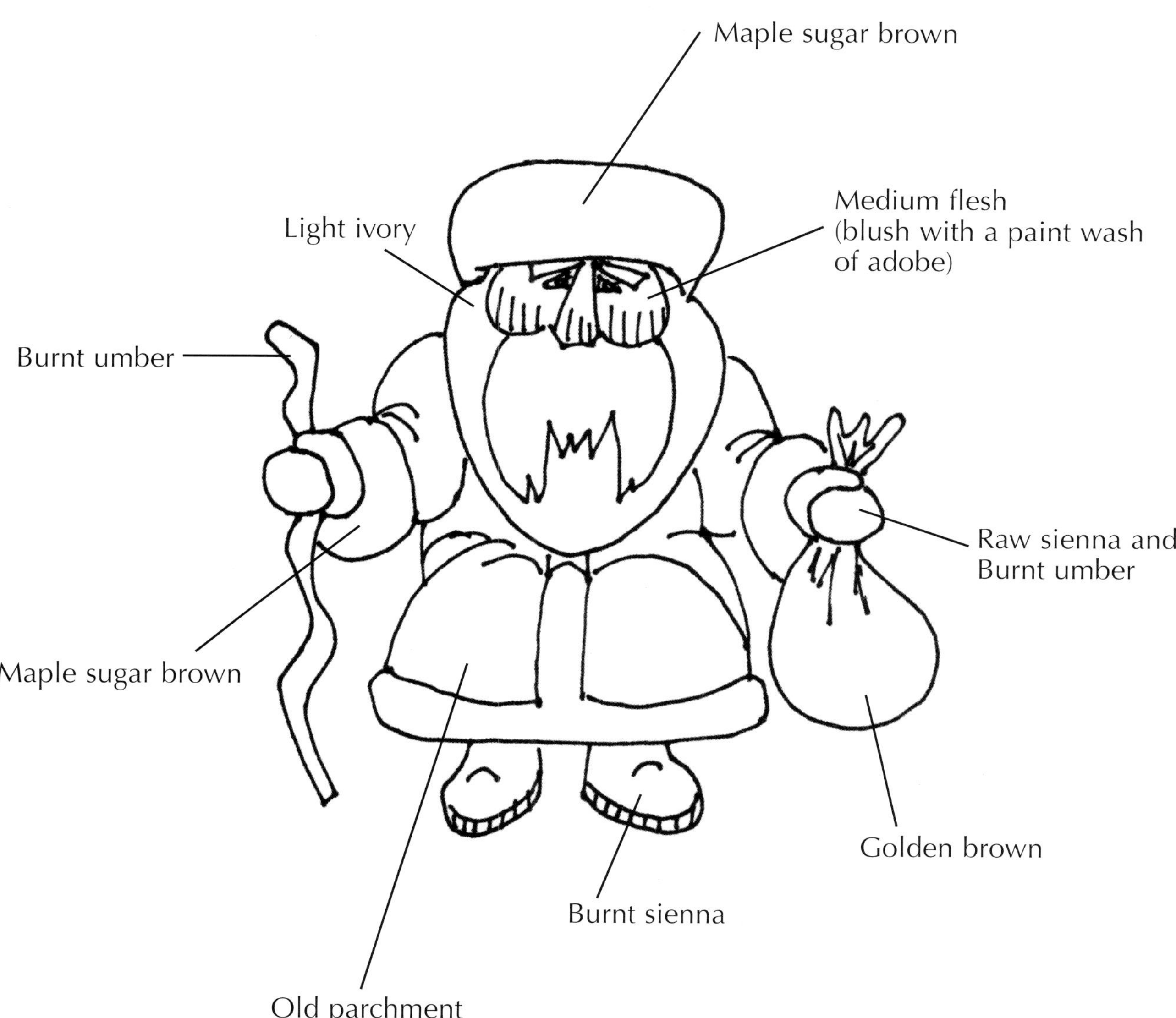
Maple sugar brown
Light ivory
Medium flesh
(blush with a paint wash
of adobe)
Burnt umber
Raw sienna and
Burnt umber
Maple sugar brown
Golden brown
Burnt sienna
Old parchment

All colors manufactured by Delta Ceramcoat® unless otherwise noted.

Pere Noel
France

Wood List

Body	1 ea.	3½" x 2" x 2"
Legs	1 ea.	⅞" x 2" x ¾"
	1 ea.	⅞" x 3" x ¾"
Arms	2 ea.	1½" x ¾" x ¾"
Boots	2 ea.	¾" x 1" x ⅝"
Doll	1 ea.	1½" x ¾" x 1"
Doll Arm	1 ea.	¾" x ½" x ⅜"
Basket	1 ea.	⅝" x 1" x ¾"
Eye Pins	4 ea.	

Colored wire for basket handle

Paint List

Adobe
Autumn brown
Brown iron oxide
Chrome green light
Cosmos blue
Americana® Country red
Empire gold
Golden brown
Ivory
Light ivory
Medium flesh
Pine green
Queen Anne's lace

Pere Noel France

The Pattern

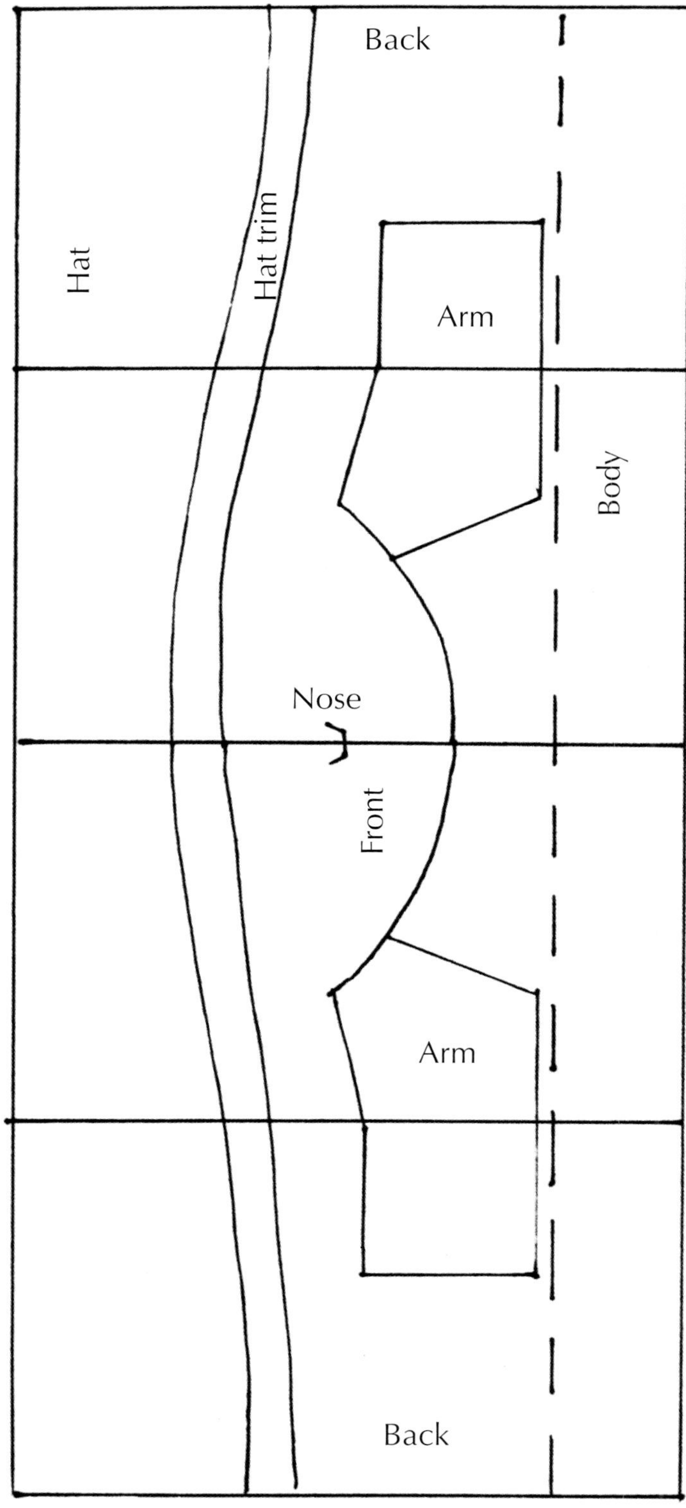
Back
Hat
Hat trim
Arm
Body
Nose
Front
Arm
Back

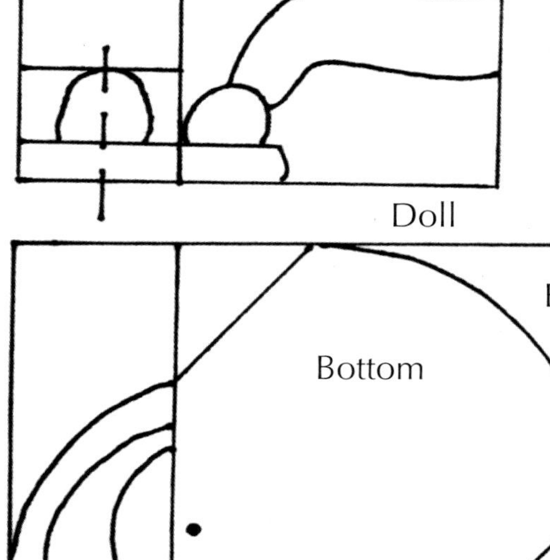
Doll

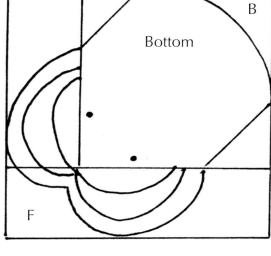

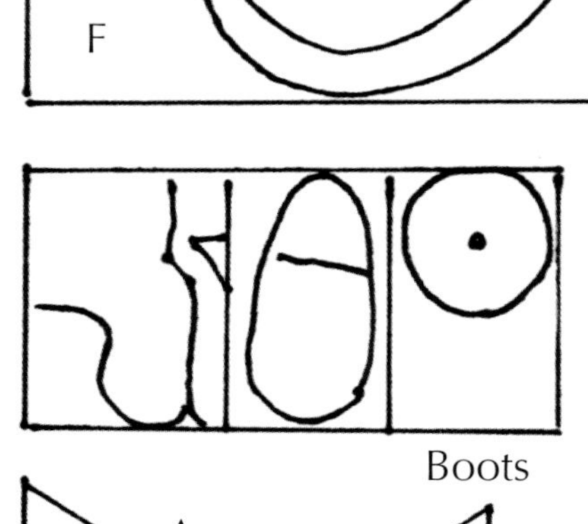
B
Bottom
F
Boots

Basket

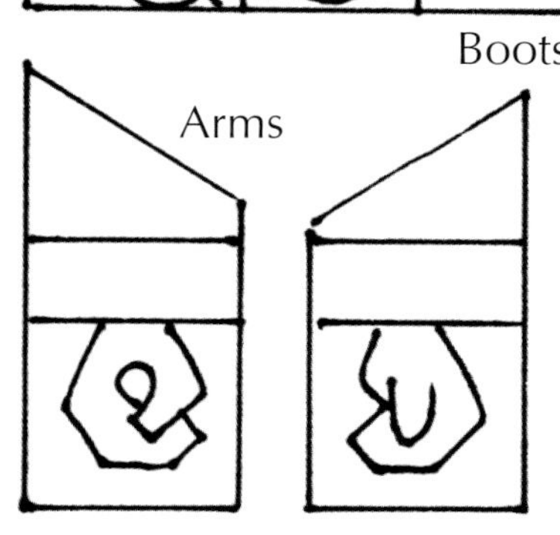
Arms

Baby's arm

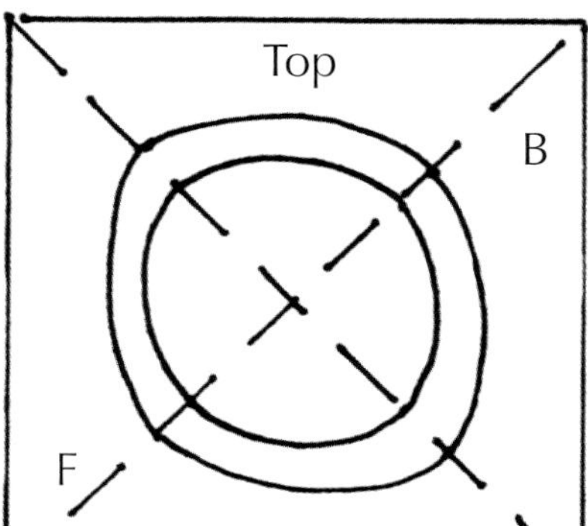
Top
B
F

Face pattern

PERE NOEL
FRANCE

THE COLOR CHART

Hat motif

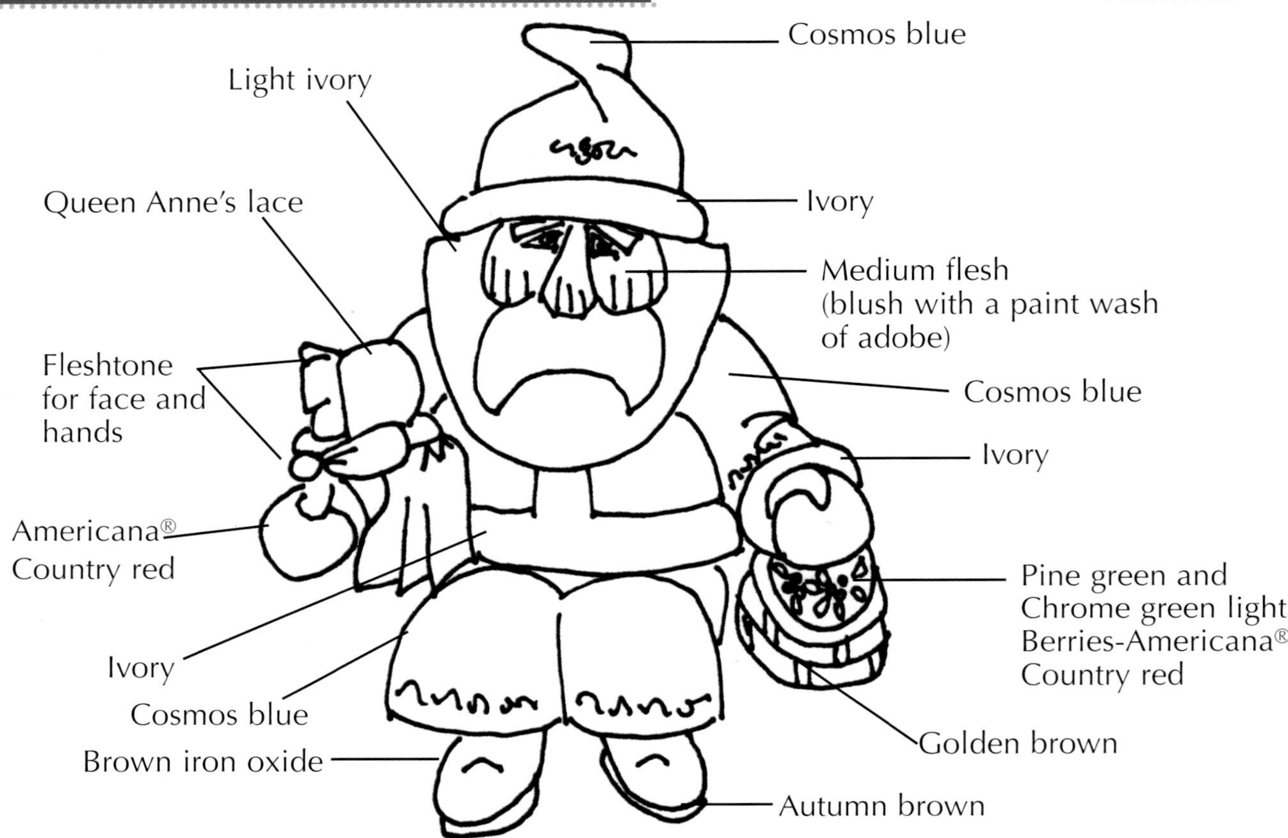
Cosmos blue
Light ivory
Queen Anne's lace
Ivory
Medium flesh
(blush with a paint wash
of adobe)
Fleshtone
for face and
hands
Cosmos blue
Ivory
Americana®
Country red
Pine green and
Chrome green light
Berries-Americana®
Country red
Ivory
Cosmos blue
Golden brown
Brown iron oxide
Autumn brown

Pant and sleeve doodad
1) Light ivory dot
2) Adobe dot
3) Empire gold dot
4) Add chrome green light leaves
5) Light ivory baby's breath
Actual size

All colors manufactured by Delta Ceramcoat® unless otherwise noted.

Sint Niklaes
Belgium

Wood List

Body	1 ea.	3" x 2" x 2"
Arms	1 ea.	1½" x ¾" x ¾"
	1 ea.	1⅛" x ¾" x ¾"
Boots	2 ea.	¾" x 1" x ⅝"
Skirt	1 ea.	⅞" x 2" x ¾"
	1 ea.	⅞" x 3" x ¾"
Bag	1 ea.	1¼" x 1" x 1"
Bag Top	1 ea.	1"x ½" x ½"
Tree	1 ea.	1¼" x ¾" x ¾"
Eye Pins	4 ea	

Paint List

Adobe
Autumn brown
Blue haze
Brown iron oxide
Chrome green light
Country (Americana) red
Empire gold
Golden brown
Pine green
Hunter green
Ivory
Light ivory
Medium flesh
Toffee

Sint Niklaes
Belgium

The Pattern

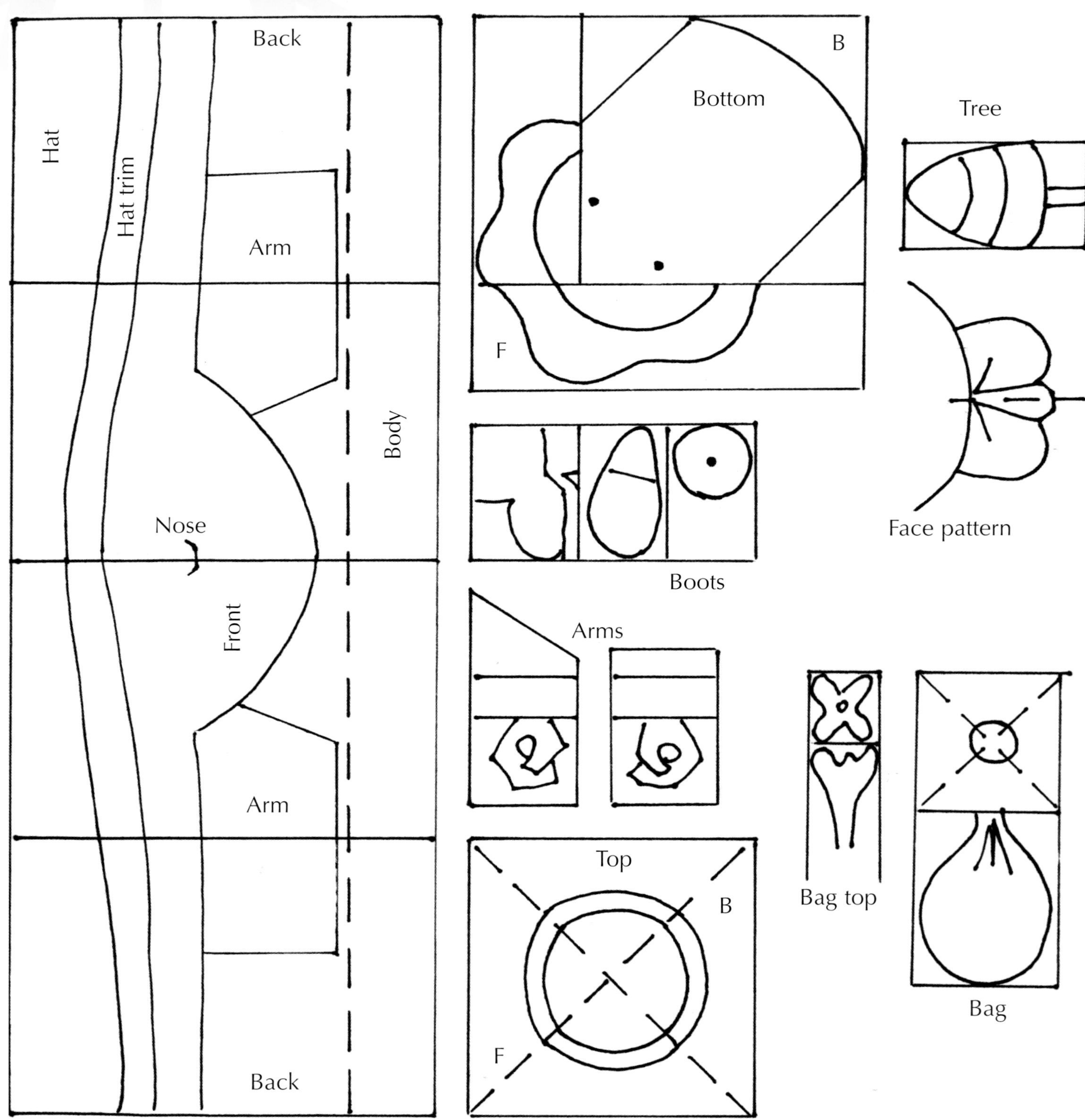
Back
Hat
Hat trim
Arm
Body
Nose
Front
Arm
Back
B
Bottom
F
Tree
Face pattern
Boots
Arms
Top
B
F
Bag top
Bag

Sint Niklaes
Belgium

The Color Chart

Hat motif

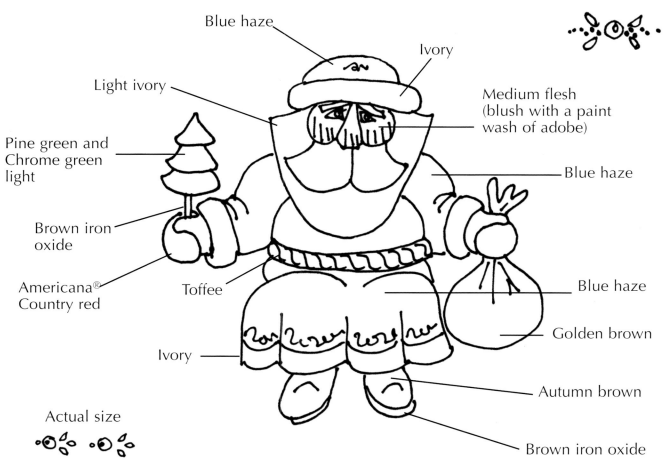

Blue haze

Ivory

Light ivory

Medium flesh
(blush with a paint
wash of adobe)

Pine green and
Chrome green
light

Blue haze

Brown iron
oxide

Americana®
Country red

Toffee

Blue haze

Golden brown

Ivory

Autumn brown

Brown iron oxide

Actual size

Robe doodad

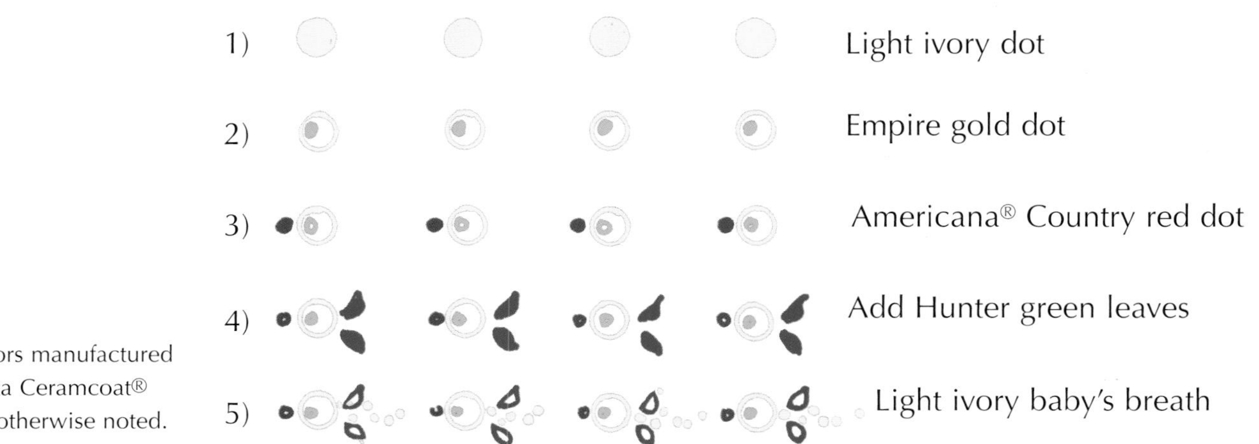

1) Light ivory dot
2) Empire gold dot
3) Americana® Country red dot
4) Add Hunter green leaves
5) Light ivory baby's breath

All colors manufactured by Delta Ceramcoat® unless otherwise noted.

Starman
Poland

Wood List

Body	1 ea.	3" x 2" x 2"
Legs	1 ea.	7/8" x 2" x 3/4"
	1 ea.	7/8" x 3" x 3/4"
Arms	2 ea.	1 1/2" x 3/4" x 3/4"
Boots	2 ea.	3/4" x 1" x 5/8"
Drum	1 ea.	1/2" x 3/4" x 3/4"
Lower Staff	1 ea.	1 1/2" x 3/8" x 3/8"
Upper Staff	1 ea.	1" x 3/8" x 3/8"
Eye Pins	4 ea.	

Colored wire for drum hanger

Paint List

Adobe
Black
Brown iron oxide
Americana® Country red
Empire gold
Hunter green
Ivory
Light ivory
Medium flesh
Metallic gold
Midnight blue
Trail tan
Western sunset

STARMAN POLAND

THE PATTERN

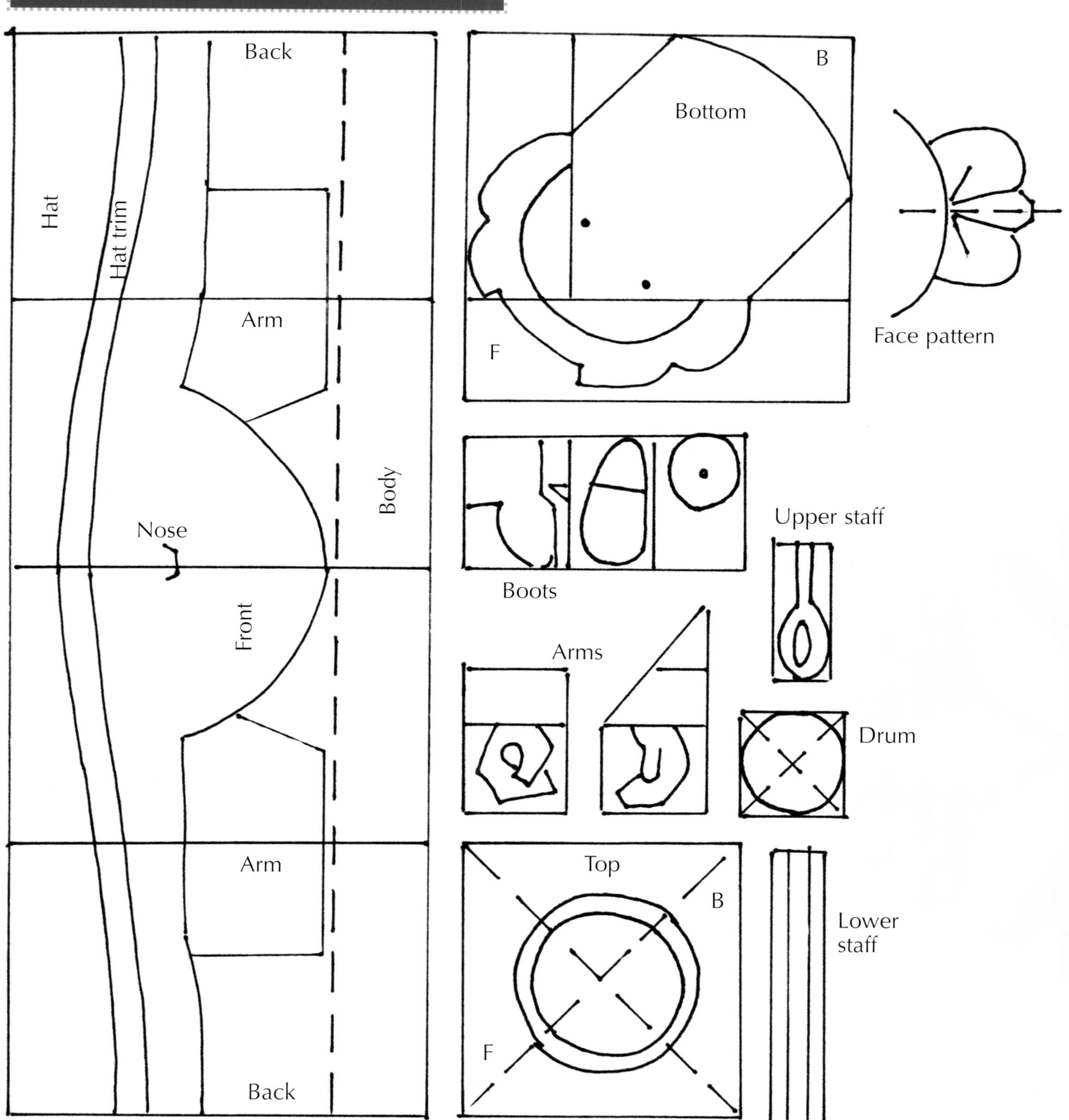
Back
Hat
Hat trim
Arm
Body
Nose
Front
Arm
Back
B
Bottom
F
Face pattern
Boots
Upper staff
Arms
Drum
Top
B
F
Lower staff

Starman
Poland

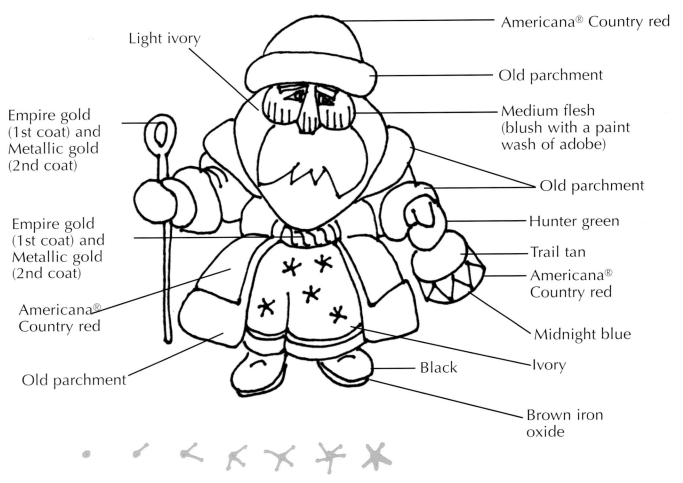

The Color Chart

Light ivory

Americana® Country red

Old parchment

Empire gold
(1st coat) and
Metallic gold
(2nd coat)

Medium flesh
(blush with a paint
wash of adobe)

Old parchment

Hunter green

Empire gold
(1st coat) and
Metallic gold
(2nd coat)

Trail tan

Americana®
Country red

Americana®
Country red

Midnight blue

Black

Ivory

Old parchment

Brown iron
oxide

Metallic gold dot with stylus
Pull out color from dot
with stylus for each ray of star

All colors manufactured by Delta Ceramcoat® unless otherwise noted.

Actual size